Volume One

STEEL ON STEEL

Bill Perkins

COMPASS INTERNATIONAL, INC.
COEUR D'ALENE, IDAHO

STEEL ON STEEL

Volume One

Compass International, Inc.
Coeur d'Alene, Idaho
www.compass.org

First Printing May 2018, Second Printing September 2018
Printed in the United States of America.

ISBN-10: 1-5743715-1-7
ISBN-13: 978-1-5743715-1-2

Cover illustration and design by Gordon McDonald, GoGo Design.

All proceeds from the purchase of this book go to Compass Int'l, Inc.

CONTENTS

CONTENTS

PREFACE

"And I, brethren, could not speak to you as to spiritual men, but as to men of flesh, as to ***infants in Christ.*** *I gave you milk to drink, not solid food; for you were not yet able to receive it. Indeed, even now you are not yet able,"* *1Cor. 3:1-2*

I've always been intrigued with the way the Bible compares new Believers to new babies. For those of us who've experienced raising babies, we know they're totally dependent on what we feed and teach them.

If we didn't feed them a balanced diet, they would not grow properly. And once they began to grow, crawl, and walk, they *really* had to be watched over to keep them out of trouble!

And the Bible tells us that's how we are to think of new Believers. We are to feed (teach) them with milk at the beginning, but then ultimately get them to eat the real meat, the deep richness of Scripture illuminating Jesus and God's instructions for living a victorious life.

Yet today, far too many churches have abandoned teaching meat-rich sermons point-blank from Scripture and instead only teach milk-toast topical teaching. The result is that those in their flock live frustrated spiritual lives as they have to operate powerless against a formidable enemy who's had 6000 years of practice.

To not teach the hard truths in the Bible means teachers are willfully ignoring the Bible's pointed calls to exhort Christians to mature in understanding God's infallible Word.

> *"...preach the word; ...reprove, rebuke, exhort, with great patience and instruction." 2Tim. 4:2*

> *"But solid food is for the mature, who because of practice have their senses trained to discern good and evil." Heb. 5:14*

God says all the church elders are to be teachers (1Tim. 3:2), but rarely do we see all the elders of a church taking their turns teaching. In that same vein of multiple teachers, God also says a wise man has many counselors. Those who teach the Bible are sinners too. And none teach everything perfectly. So we're to have several sources of input.

> *"Where there is no guidance the people fall, but in abundance of counselors there is victory." Prov. 11:14*

And the purpose of any teacher or counselor is to point you to verses in the Bible. That's why for the first 1900 years of the Church, most people went to their pastor for counseling, to find a verse or two that shed light on the problem or solution at hand.

> *"Your testimonies also are my delight; They are my counselors." Psa. 119:24*

Compass was created in 1993 to offer additional teachers for the serious Believer who wanted more than milk to eat (1Cor. 3:1-2) and who desired to dig deeper into the far depths of the Word in order to better understand the richness of Scripture, the hidden things of our Creator God.

> *"It is the glory of God to conceal a matter, but the glory of kings is to search out a matter." Prov. 25:2*

As Believers, we're adopted into royalty (Rev. 1:6) and will ultimately live and reign with Him (Rev. 20:4). So here we are, in this life, with this incredibly valuable resource available to us—God's inerrant Word—yet fewer and fewer seek its valuable instruction.

Think about it—the Bible says every book, every chapter, every word of every sentence in the Bible is supernaturally inspired by God. God inspired, God breathed, all 70 books of the Bible we have today.

Take that last remark as a case in point—just how many books are in the Bible? Most say 66, not 70. But if you dig into your Bible, you learn the number seven is always used by God as His number for completion.

So should we just assume we have only 66 and not 70?

The answer for those who dig deeper is that Psalms is actually five books, not one. If you look at Psalm 42, in most Bibles it says, "Book 2." Psalms 73 says "Book 3." Psalms 90 says "Book 4." And Psalms 107 says "Book 5." So there *are* 70 books of the Bible. It's fully complete and nothing else can be added.

Those 70 books of Godly inspired text are communications sent to us as His trustworthy instructions of how to live in this life. Therefore it's incumbent on us to armor up with Biblical armor, what we call *Steel On Steel.*

> *"Iron sharpens iron, so one man sharpens another."*
> *Prov. 27:17*

Steeling our minds with Biblical truth in order to be used by the Lord in our lives is Compass' mission. And when you have multiple teachers, sometimes you may hear something new. So you must look hard to see if it stands the Berean Scriptural test of Acts 17:11.

> *"Now these were more noble-minded than those in Thessalonica, for they received the word with great eagerness, examining the Scriptures daily to see whether these things were so." Acts 17:11*

So Bible study is critical for Biblical maturity. To fully understand our Creator God, what He wants us to have as goals in our lives and how we are to live in this world, we must dig and dissect God's infallible Word. So 25 years ago we started Compass to look deeply into Scripture to best armor us for the days in which we live. Whether it's Bible prophecy, apologetics, doctrine, finances or understanding how to make the best decisions in these times, we know God's Truth sheds glorious light in every area.

The Bible has a wealth of amazing topics from which to armor ourselves for this day and hour. It's late in the game and Satan has come out of the shadows. No longer subtle, his actions are that of a desperado, wishing to take with him to eternal hell everyone he can.

Therefore, our prayer is that the "steel on steel" in this book will challenge you to think about what you believe and why you believe it. We want you to be sure your doctrines, the things that drive and guide your understanding of God's inerrant Word, are defendable. We want you to have solid arguments to defend the accuracy of every Word God inspired.

> *"...always being ready...to give an account for the hope that is in you," 1Pet 3:15*

So enjoy this eye-opening STEEL ON STEEL!

Note: All Scripture quotations are taken from the *New American Standard Bible* (NASB), and emphasis has been added by the author where underlined or bolded.

THANK YOU, LORD...

...for these who have helped so much in making this book possible — Susie, Tracy, Gordon, Katie, Willow, Jeff, Penny, John, Walt, Joc, Shawn, Tammy, Adam, Marlin, Connie, Daryl, Ken, Andy, Kenny, Lois, David and our awesome Compass Pointes!

CHAPTER ONE

TEN UNMISTAKABLE SIGNS WE'RE IN THE LAST OF THE LAST DAYS

Today things are moving so fast it's helpful to just step back, take a breath and look at the numerous Bible prophecies being fulfilled all around us. Here are ten fulfilled prophecies that should convince anyone with two brain cells that we're definitely living in the last of the last days!

1) Israel Is Back In Her Homeland

"Say to them, 'Thus says the Lord GOD, "Behold, I will take the sons of Israel from among the nations where they have gone, and I will gather them from every side and bring them into their own land;" Ezek. 37:21

THE PALESTINE POST

CARL MARX

STATE OF ISRAEL IS BORN

Most Crowded Hours in Palestine's History

JEWS TAKE OVER SECURITY ZONES

Egyptian Air Force Spitfires Bomb Tel Aviv; One Shot Down

U.S. RECOGNIZES JEWISH STATE

Proclamation by Head Of Government

2 Columns Cross Southern Border

Etzion Settlers Taken P.O.W.

Special Assembly Adjourns

Bible prophecies regarding the latter days begin and end with Israel. Until God regathered Israel back to her homeland in 1948, most latter-days prophecies could not begin. But return they did. In the late 1800s, after almost 2000 years of worldwide dispersion, the Jews began filtering back to their original God-given land.

In 1917, at the end of WWI, the Balfour Agreement gave the Jews a legal right of return. And on May 14, 1948, the United Nations declared Israel a sovereign nation.

2) Israel Is A World Problem

> *"It will come about in that day that I will make Jerusalem a heavy stone for all the peoples; all who lift it will be severely injured. And all the nations of the earth will be gathered against it." Zech. 12:3*

The Bible not only promised that Israel would return to her God-given land but that this tiny nation would also become a burdensome stone to the world. Hardly a day goes by that Israel's not in the news. Israel has a population of about 8 million, the Arabs about 450 million. You can barely see Israel in the middle of a Muslim dominated land.

Every American administration since Israel became a nation in 1948 has tried and failed to secure a lasting peace in the Middle East. The national news has a continuous dribble of problems regarding Israel and the Middle East, usually making Israel out to be the cause of the problem.

This ultimately ends with every nation on earth coming against Israel in the seven-year Tribulation Period. Toward the end of the Tribulation period, the Antichrist will bring together the world's armies to "kill the Jews." But their Messiah, Jesus of Nazareth, will return to earth and save them from annihilation.

3) Homosexual Perversion

"For the coming of the Son of Man will be just like the days of Noah." Matt. 24:37

> ***"Sex is front-page copy everywhere. (But) nothing can alter the fact that God calls perversion sin."***
> ***— Billy Graham***

The Bible says that the days before the Rapture will be "just like" the days before God destroyed the earth with a global flood and also just like the days before He destroyed Sodom and Gommorah. One of the distinguishing characteristics specifically mentioned was widespread homosexual sin. God will again judge homosexual sin in the future.

"...and they called to Lot and said to him, 'Where are the men who came to you tonight? Bring them out to us that we may have relations [intercourse] *with them.'" Gen 19:5*

"It was the same as happened in the days of Lot: they were eating, they were drinking, they were buying, they were selling, they were planting, they were building; but on the day that Lot went out from Sodom it rained fire and brimstone from heaven and destroyed them all. It will be just the same on the day that the Son of Man is revealed." Luke 17:28-30

Always know that homosexual behavior is sin. Homosexuals are not born that way, rather they choose to be.

Always know that homosexual behavior *is* sin. Homosexuals are not born that way, rather they *choose* to be. Much like a thief can't stop stealing without the transcending power of God, a homosexual can't repent or turn from his or her sin without the power of God. Murder, stealing, adultery, homosexuality, etc., *are* clearly defined as *sin* by God's Word. God defines sin, not the government!

Today, homosexual rights are on the front burner of the politically correct push to bring this perversion out into the open as normal, incorrectly equating their demands with the push for black civil rights in the '60s.

But comparing homosexual rights to civil rights is not an apples-to-apples comparison because homosexual behavior is a choice and black skin color isn't. That fact seems to be lost in the rhetoric as God-given and constitutionally protected rights of Christians are tossed out the window while homosexual perversion is elevated to "normal" status.

4) A Cashless Society

> *"And he causes all, the small and the great, and the rich and the poor, and the free men and the slaves, to be given a mark on their right hand or on their forehead, and he provides that no one will be able to buy or to sell, except the one who has the mark, either the name of the beast or the number of his name." Rev. 13:16-17*

A recent survey said only 10% of Americans always carry cash. The worldwide movement toward electronic payments has been breathtaking. For most of those reading this book, if our bank unexpectedly froze our accounts, we'd be in deep trouble.

With our worldwide banking system, we're obviously not too far from one person literally being able to control the world. And that's where we're headed... to a point where one person will have total control of all transactions on earth.

5) Russian / Iranian Coalition

> *"Son of man, set your face toward Gog of the land of Magog, the prince of Rosh, Meshech and Tubal, and prophesy against him." Ezek. 38:2*

"I will turn you about and put hooks into your jaws, and I will bring you out, and all your army, horses and horsemen, all of them splendidly attired, a great company with buckler and shield, all of them wielding swords; Persia, Ethiopia and Put [Libya in some translations] *with them, all of them with shield and helmet;" Ezek. 38:4,5*

"After many days you will be summoned; in the latter years you will come into the land that is restored from the sword, whose inhabitants have been gathered from many nations to the mountains of Israel which had been a continual waste; but its people were brought out from the nations, and they are living securely, all of them." Ezek. 38:8

Amazingly, 2700 years ago the Bible predicted that Gog/Rosh (modern-day Russia) will invade Israel from the north with Persia (modern-day Iran) as one of her principal allies. So it's not surprising that today Russia and Iran are becoming so close militarily.

Also keep in mind that the above prophecies pinpoint this time to be after Israel comes back into her land in the latter days.

6) Nuclear Weapons

"And another, a red horse, went out; and to him who sat on it, it was granted to take peace from the earth, and that men would slay one another; and a great sword was given to him." Rev. 6:4

"Now this will be the plague with which the LORD will strike all the peoples who have gone to war against Jerusalem; their flesh will rot while they stand on their feet, and their eyes will rot in their sockets, and their tongue will rot in their mouth." Zech. 14:12

How would you have described a neutron bomb 2,500 years ago? John and Zechariah had to do just that! All they knew was that it was huge and quite destructive! So destructive that flesh melted off their bodies before their bones hit the ground! That sounds exactly like a neutron bomb that's designed to vaporize the people and leave the buildings intact.

7) Increase of Knowledge

"But as for you, Daniel, conceal these words and seal up the book until the end of time; many will go back and forth, and knowledge will increase." Dan. 12:4

"The chariots race madly in the streets, they rush wildly in the squares, their appearance is like torches, they dash to and fro like lightning flashes." Nah. 2:4

The Internet has become the modern-day purveyor of information, as people pretty much have access to anything and everything at their fingertips.

Ease of local or worldwide transportation by car, plane, train or ship is considered normal. Nahum 2:4 reads like the prophet is looking down on a busy intersection at night.

8) Mockers Denying Jesus' Second Coming

> *"Know this first of all, that in the last days mockers will come with their mocking, following after their own lusts, and saying, 'Where is the promise of His coming? For ever since the fathers fell asleep, all continues just as it was from the beginning of creation.'" 2Pet. 3:3,4*

Denying the clear Biblical doctrines of the Lord first returning in the Rapture is a *sign* of the Rapture. The dispensational model for Scripture interpretation is the only consistent way to know what God says to us in His written Word.

Yet over 80% of the "Christian Church" in the world are Amillennial in their theology, which is a basic denial of the Rapture. (See inside cover for Dispensation Chart.)

Notice this is not a verse talking about non-Christians; because it mentions "fathers" and God's "creation," it's referring to Christians living in the last days!

9) 144,000 Jewish Evangelists Identified

"And I heard the number of those who were sealed, one hundred and forty-four thousand sealed from every tribe of the sons of Israel:" Rev. 7:4

"And they sang a new song before the throne and before the four living creatures and the elders; and no one could learn the song except the one hundred and forty-four thousand who had been purchased from the earth. These are the ones who have not been defiled with women, for they have kept themselves chaste. These are the ones who follow the Lamb wherever He goes. These have been purchased from among men as first fruits to God and to the Lamb." Rev. 14:3,4

This puzzling prophecy says God will choose 144,000 Jewish men and reveal Himself to them on Mount Zion in Jerusalem (different from the Mount of Olives and Mount Moriah). Most interestingly, these men are virgins. They are Ultra-Orthodox Jews, or *Haredi* in Hebrew, and are discussed in greater detail in Chapter 15.

10) Israel's Deserts Blooming

"In the days to come Jacob will take root, Israel will blossom and sprout, and they will fill the whole world with fruit." Is. 27:6

Jordan River 1913

"The wilderness and the desert will be glad, and the Arabah [desert] *will rejoice and blossom; Like the crocus it will blossom profusely." Is. 35:1,2*

The Bible prophesies that the parched and desert land of Israel will bloom profusely.

In the late 1800s, Mark Twain made the long trip to Israel and commented:

> *"..... A desolate country whose soil is rich enough, but is given over wholly to weeds... a silent mournful expanse.... a desolation.... we never saw a human being on the whole route.... hardly a tree or shrub anywhere. Even the olive tree and the cactus, those fast friends of a worthless soil, had almost deserted the country." (Innocents Abroad,* Mark Twain, 1867*)*

Jordan River Today

The Turks of Ottoman Empire who controlled the land for 400 years had heavily taxed trees on property in Israel. So most people cut down all their trees to avoid paying the tax!

Since the Jews began returning to their homeland in earnest in the late 1800s, the Jewish National Fund has planted over 250 million trees throughout the country (Israel is roughly the size of Vermont).

One of the most amazing things we see in Israel today on our Bible trips is the incredible and colorful blooming vegetation in the Jordan Valley and around the Dead Sea—the lowest point on earth.

The drip irrigation system, developed by Israel, allows her to export $65 million in dates each year from palm trees grown around the void-of-moisture Dead Sea.

The drip system enables as little as a cupful of water to bountifully nourish a whole tree for a day. Using this method in the desert has literally caused it to bloom in the last 50 years. They now export fresh fruit and vegetables via plane to Europe every day but Saturday (Shabbat).

Ten prophecies have been explained, but here is a "bonus" prophecy that may be the next to be fulfilled:

11) Israel Discovering Great Riches

> *"Sheba and Dedan and the merchants of Tarshish with all its villages will say to you, 'Have you come to capture spoil? Have you assembled your company to seize plunder, to carry away silver and gold, to take away cattle and goods, to capture great spoil?'" Ezek. 38:13*

The Bible says there will be great riches discovered in the land of Israel. The riches are so great that sovereign nations band together to invade and capture the riches. This is unfolding before our eyes!

Israel has discovered huge gas fields inland and offshore her coasts. And as they say in Texas, "Where there's gas, there's oil." So it's only a matter of time.

Over 500 oil wells had been drilled in Israel to no avail. But recently Israel struck oil in the Galilee area, and it's a whopper. It's over 10 times the average size of oil wells in the world and will provide billions of gallons of oil a year, far exceeding the needs of Israel (https://www.rt.com/business/317906-oil-golan-heights-israel/).

As more wells are tapped into this massive reserve, Israel will become a major oil supplier to Europe and North America. Do you think this will sit well with the Arabs? They already seethe at Israel's success in rebuilding a great nation in only 70 years. They're going to go bonkers!

And the prophecy also mentions gold and silver riches. As the Dead Sea dries up, could it expose more and more unseen riches? Trust me, when Israel is able to supply oil at a lower price from a closer delivery point (the eastern edge of the Mediterranean Sea), the Muslims will go nuts.

And if Israel also discovers gold and silver, the Arabs will wet their collective pants. So Israel's discovering great riches is closely tied into prophecy #2 above, Israel being a burdening stone to the world!

To a trusting-the-blood Believer, seeing so much Bible prophecy coming together should be an exciting incentive to ask the Lord for His wisdom for being sensitive to the leading of His Spirit to reach our lost family, friends and co-workers with the Good News. And Good News it is!

CHAPTER TWO

WHY ASKING JESUS INTO YOUR HEART WON'T SAVE YOU

This truth is a shocker to a lot of people!

If you have the opportunity to witness to people and God convicts them of their sin and their need for a savior, what do you tell them to do to become Christians? Many people will tell a non-believer that they need to pray the sinner's prayer and "ask Jesus into your heart."

Where is *that* in the Bible?

It's not. There is no place in the Bible that non-believers are instructed to ask Jesus into their heart to save them. And no place in the Bible says that if you do ask Jesus into your heart you will be saved. But, unfortunately, this non-Biblical tactic has grown to be the norm.

So what does the Bible say? Let's look at some verses.

The Philippian jailer asked Paul, "What must I do to be saved?" Paul answered,

"Believe on the Lord Jesus Christ and you will be saved." Acts 16:30-31

The key word in Paul's answer is "believe." In the original Greek, the word "believe" (*pisteuo*) means "to have faith in" or "to trust in." It's in the aorist tense in the Greek, which means it doesn't require future action, just a single decision.

The late Dr. Lewis Sperry Chafer said in his book *Salvation: God's Marvelous Work of Grace* (p.33), "This one word 'believe' represents all a sinner can do and all a sinner must do to be saved."

Chafer's statement is Biblically consistent. Consider these verses:

"...whoever believes in Him..." John 3:16

"He who believes in the Son..." John 3:36

"...he who hears My word, and believes..." John 5:24

...he who believes in Me will never thirst." John 6:35

"...everyone who ... believes in Him..." John 6:40

"...he who believes has eternal life." John 6:47

"...unless you believe..." John 8:24

"...he who believes in Me..." John 11:25

"...everyone who ... believes in Me..." John 11:26

"... that [by] *believing you may have life..." John 20:31*

You don't have to pray a prayer or ask Jesus into your heart to be saved. You simply have to *believe* that you are a sinner, incapable of saving yourself, and that God sent His only Son to the earth to shed His blood, die for your sins and be resurrected, defeating death. You are, by faith alone, trusting God and His written Word to be true.

The "Gospel" or "good news" that you must "believe" centers on Jesus Christ, the Son of God, who died for our sins and rose again.

"Now I make known to you, brethren, the gospel which I preached to you, which also you received, in which also you stand, by which also you are saved ... that Christ died for our sins according to the Scriptures, and that He was buried, and that He was raised on the third day according to the Scriptures." 1Cor. 15:1-4

The "Gospel," or "good news," that you must *believe* centers on Jesus Christ, the Son of God, who died for our sins and rose again. The Gospel does not include "praying for Jesus to come into your heart."

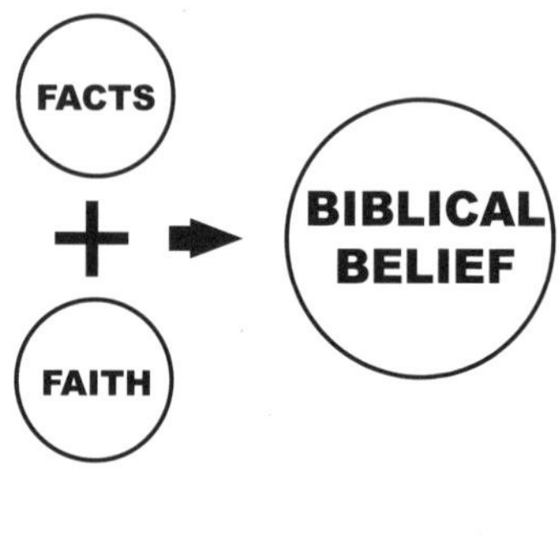

It is, of course, possible that someone "walked the aisle" or prayed the infamous "sinner's prayer" and *did* understand the Gospel—thereby being saved. But it was belief in the Gospel that saved, not walking the aisle, praying a prayer or asking Jesus into his/her heart.

And it is just as possible that there are many who have a false salvation security based on praying a prayer for Jesus to come into their heart without understanding the Gospel!

But what about the verses about God living in us?

"...Which is Christ in you..." Col. 1:27

"...Christ lives in me..." Gal. 2:20

"Because you are sons, God has sent forth the Spirit of His Son into our hearts..." Gal. 4:6

Yes, every Believer has Jesus living in his or her heart. But how did He get there? God came into our hearts at salvation, the exact moment we, by faith, *believed* the Gospel.

We don't ask Him to come in; He comes in because we believe.

"But as many as received Him, to them He gave the right to become children of God, even to those who believe in His name," John 1:12

"In Him, you also, after listening to the message of truth, the gospel of your salvation - having also believed, you were sealed in Him with the Holy Spirit of promise," Eph. 1:13

"We have confused the means of salvation with the results of salvation."
— Dennis Rosker

First we believe, then God sends His Spirit into our hearts. To tell someone to "ask Jesus into your heart" is blatantly skipping the Scripturally necessary "believing in" / "trusting in" the Gospel.

Dennis Rosker said it best in his book *Seven Reasons Not To Ask Jesus Into Your Heart.* He stated, "We have confused the means of salvation with the results of salvation."

But what about Revelation 3:20?

"Behold, I stand at the door and knock; if anyone hears My voice and opens the door, I will come in to him and will dine with him, and he with Me." Rev. 3:20

Notably absent from this verse are the words "ask," "Jesus," and "your heart."

If this verse is written to Believers, the context is about Jesus desiring to be number one in their lives, as they had confused earthly success with spiritual maturity. Jesus desired the Laodiceans to make Him not only Savior but also predominate in their lives.

Many have misunderstood the phrase "I will come into him" to mean "come into their heart." Michael Cocoris discusses the Greek words used in Rev. 3:20 in his book *Evangelism, A Biblical Approach.* He says "Christ will come 'in to' (two different Greek words), not 'into' (one Greek word). The verse is saying that Christ will come in the church to the person, not that Christ will come into the person." Cocoris later adds, "Christ is speaking of fellowship, not salvation."

Jesus wants a moment-by-moment fellowship with Believers.

> *"... taking every thought captive to the obedience of Christ," 2Cor. 10:5*

However, if this verse is written to non-Believers, as John MacArthur contends, the phrase "standing at the door" does not mean the door of your heart but rather the door of the Laodicean Church.

MacArthur states in his *Commentary on the Book of Revelation* (page 140): "The door on which Christ is knocking is not the door to a single human heart, but to the Laodicean Church."

MacArthur believes these people held to their own form of Godliness but were denying the power of the Holy Spirit (2Tim 3:5). Therefore, regardless of whether Revelation 3:20 was addressing Believers or non-Believers, it is not a verse instructing us that we need to ask Jesus into our hearts to be saved. It's just not there.

Two quotes from Charles Ryrie from his book *So Great Salvation*:

> *"...it seems to me that those who believe in the inerrancy of the Bible ought to be especially concerned with accuracy in communicating the truth."*

> *"Just as words were the means God used to record the Gospel in the Scriptures, so words are the means we use to explain the Gospel to others. Therefore, a correct choice of words is important, even essential, in stating the Gospel well."*

"It is not faith that saves you, but rather the object of your faith."

There may be someone reading this who prayed a "come into my heart" prayer and your faith of salvation is in the fact you prayed the prayer. Or you may have walked to the front of a meeting and your faith is in the fact you walked forward. **It's not faith that saves you, but rather the object of your faith.** Your faith or belief must be in the Biblical Gospel of Jesus Christ, not faith or belief in your good works, a denomination or a false god.

If there is any doubt that you are a Christian, simply believe by faith in the true Gospel of salvation—that God sent His Son Jesus to die for your personal sins and raised Him from the dead, defeating death so you can have eternal life with God.

If you truly believe that, God's Holy Spirit will immediately come into your life and change you forever. You'll be what the Bible refers to as a "Born-Again" Believer (John 3:1-7). God's Spirit living in you will illuminate Scripture (1Cor. 2:10-13) and convict you of sin (John 16:8).

Salvation has zero to do with what you did in the past—or will do in the future—and everything to do with what Jesus did on the Cross 2000 years ago. When you believe, you are forever assured of eternal life with Jesus because once He comes into your life, He's there forever (Heb. 13:5).

CHAPTER THREE

THE MYSTERY OF THE CHURCH AGE

"...the mystery which has been hidden from the past ages and generations." Col. 1:26

The word mystery in the Greek is "*mysterion,*" and it means "truth undiscoverable except by divine revelation." We have the divine Holy Spirit living in us so we should be able to understand deep truths.

The Bible mentions several mysteries in the New Testament epistles, such as:

The Mystery of the Rapture. 1Cor. 15:51

The Mystery of God coming in the flesh. Col. 2:2,3,9

The Mystery of Israel's unbelief. Rom. 11:25

The Mystery of the Antichrist. 2Thes. 2:6-10

The Mystery of Gentile inclusion in God's promises. Eph. 3:3-6

But the mystery of all mysteries is the mystery of the Church Age.

"...the mystery which for ages has been hidden." Eph. 3:9

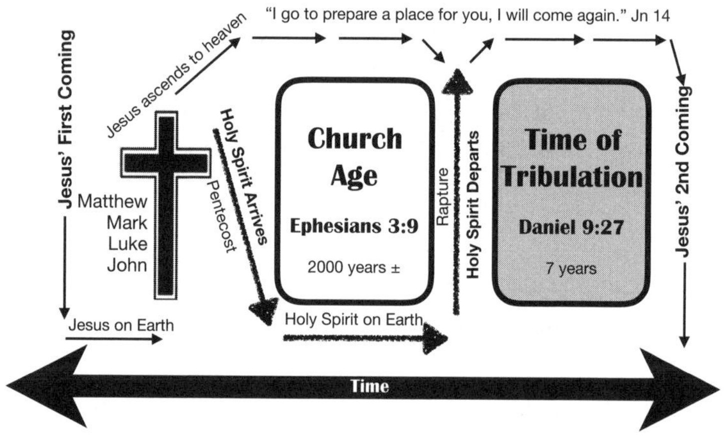

To best understand the Church Age "mystery," we need to start with God's foundational purpose for sacrifices. Mankind is born sinful and separated from God because the penalty for sin is death.

"For the wages [penalty] *of sin is death." Rom. 6:23*

Therefore, in the Old Testament God provided a way to temporarily cover man's sin via an animal blood sacrifice so that He could fellowship with man. Blood is the key. Our life depends on our blood.

"For the life of the flesh is in the blood, and I have given it to you on the altar to make atonement for your

> *souls; for* ***it is the blood*** *by reason of the life* ***that makes atonement.****" Lev. 17:11*

> *"And according to the Law, one may almost say, all things are cleansed with blood, and* ***without shedding of blood there is no forgiveness.****" Heb. 9:22*

Blood is an amazing thing. We can't live without it. Each human has about five gallons of constantly circulating blood. It's composed of red blood cells for carrying oxygen to the tissues, white blood cells for fighting infections and platelets that cause the blood to clot.

God even commanded Noah to not eat blood.

> *"Every moving thing that is alive shall be food for you; I give all to you, as I gave the green plant. Only you shall not eat flesh with its life, that is, its blood." Gen. 9:3-4*

Paul was chosen to explain this "Good News" to the world... that a great "mystery" had been revealed.

So the first thing Noah did when his family walked off the ark after the flood was to make a blood sacrifice to cover their sins (Gen. 8:20). This necessity of shedding blood to atone for man's sin (Lev. 17:11) was later incorporated into the Levitical law (Lev. 16).

So for over 1500 years God's Law demanded, and the Israelites furnished, blood sacrifices. Then, as prophesied, the Lord God came in the flesh and shed His blood on the cross as a permanent sacrifice (Eph. 1:7), ending the necessity of sacrifices for sin.

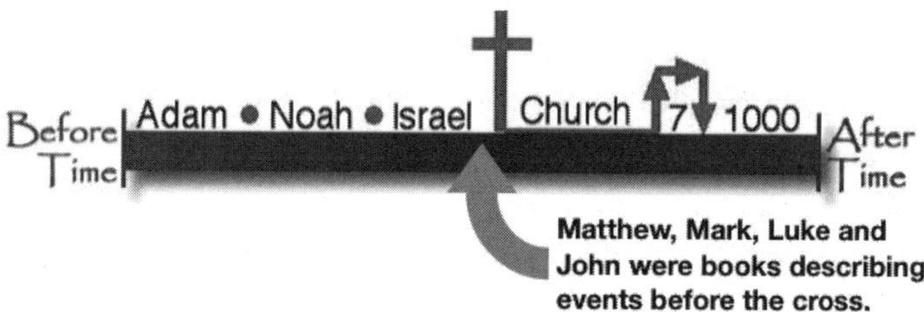

Saul (Paul) of Tarsus was chosen to explain this "Good News" to the world ... that a great "mystery" had been revealed ... that Jehovah God no longer demanded blood sacrifices because all sin had been "paid in full" by Jesus on the Cross (Col. 2:13-14). Now God the Spirit was able to come to earth to permanently indwell born-again Believers (2Cor. 1:22).

God's Spirit coming to the earth ushered in a completely new time period we call the Church Age. The Age of Israel ended with Jesus' death on the Cross. Then some 50 days later the Church Age began with a distinct purpose and destiny. The Church Age will end when God's Spirit departs at the Rapture. So the coming of the Holy Spirit and the departure of the Holy Spirit are the bookends of the Church Age.

This new time period, referred to as a Dispensation, was a complete surprise to the Jews living at the time of Christ. They were correctly reading all the verses in the Bible about the Lord sending a Messiah to conquer their enemies and rule the earth from a throne in Jerusalem.

But the Holy Spirit had not revealed to the Jews, at that time, the deep meanings behind Isaiah 53 and the suffering Messiah who had to come first.

When God said He blinded the Jewish race, it was an understatement.

And because Believers' sins were paid for by Jesus' shed blood on the Cross, making them sanctified, God could now send His Holy Spirit to indwell Believers even while they still lived in their sinful earthly containers. That was quite a shocker for the Jews.

Even today, if you want to mix it up with a Rabbinical Jew at the Wailing Wall, tell one you have God living in your heart. It makes them fighting mad because they fully understand man's sinfulness.

The Jews know they need a Messiah. They just don't think He's come yet. One of the jokes among the secular guides in Israel is that when the Messiah comes, the first question they'll ask is whether or not He's been here before.

The problem, of course, is that God has blinded the eyes and hardened the hearts of the Jewish race from receiving understanding about the mystery.

"He has blinded their eyes and He hardened their heart, so that they would not see with their eyes and percieve with their heart, and be converted, and I heal them." John 12:40

"For I do not want you, brethren, to be uninformed of this mystery—so that you be not be wise in your own estimation—that a partial hardening has happened to Israel until the fullness of the Gentiles has come in;" Rom. 11:25

When God said He blinded the Jewish race, it was an understatement. We have non-Christian Jewish guides in Israel who lead us all over the Holyland pointing out where the miracles of Jesus took place. They routinely quote chapter and verse using the New Testament as a resource.

But even though they say the words, they can't make the connection. One time a guide said, "This is where I think Jesus rose from the dead."

So I asked him if he thought Jesus was the Messiah, and he said, "No."

I continued, "Do you think Jesus ever lied?" "No, never." the guide responded. I said, "Well, Jesus claimed to be God. Do you think He is God?" He said, "No."

Smiling I said, "Then you think Jesus is a liar." "No, no, no." the guide protested. "Then you think Jesus is God?" "No, no, no!" Round and round we went.

Being content to use this kind of circular reasoning is possible only because the Jews are blinded by God from understanding the truth.

So the "mystery" remains unsolved with the Jew but is made known to the Gentile. Just as God predicted!

> *"I will sow her for Myself in the land. I will also have compassion on her who had not obtained compassion, and **I will say to those who were not My people, 'You are My people!'** And they will say, 'You are my God!'"*
> *Hos. 2:23*

Amazing! So when you're talking to a Jew, always be respectful because even though they *are* chosen by God, most are also blinded by God until the Rapture!

And it's only by the Grace of God that we're given spiritual wisdom and knowledge!

> *"...attaining to all the wealth that comes from the full assurance of understanding, resulting in a true knowledge of God's mystery, that is, Christ Himself, in whom are hidden all the treasures of wisdom and knowledge.*
> *Col. 2:2,3*

Thank you, Lord, for the things we don't deserve!!

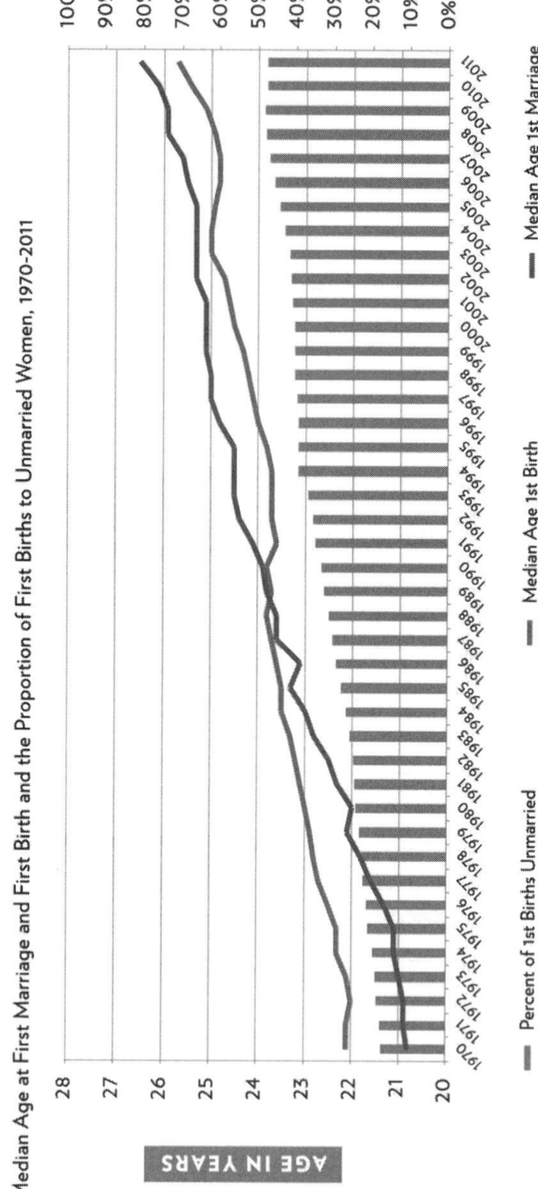

SOURCES: *National Center for Family & Marriage Research. Median age at first marriage, Current Population Survey, 1970-2011 (March Supplement); median age at first birth and percentage of first births to unmarried mothers, National Vital Statistics Reports, 1970-2011.*

CHAPTER FOUR

AMERICA'S BIRTHRATE NIGHTMARE

The following is a simple look at one of Satan's biggest worldwide coups. He's literally snuffing the life out of millions of God's creative best—the pinnacle of God's six days of creation—the human race.

Statistics show a major change has been taking place since 1970. In 1970, the average age of a woman getting married was about 20 years old, and children followed a year or two later (see chart, page 30).

But since 1970, women have been waiting longer and longer to get married. Today, the average age of a woman getting married is about 27.

And the heartbreak today is that in the U.S., the average age of the first child born to a couple is two years *older* than the marriage. Most couples get pregnant before marriage.

In Europe they see no value in marriage. They even have a "Five-Year Marriage" certificate where they commit to only a few years at a time and predetermine how to split money and any kids at the end of five years.

The U.S. is not far behind. As we move further and further from Biblical values, births to unmarried women continue to climb in America also. For example, 47% of Millennials today were born outside of marriage!

What was the main thing that changed our thinking? Birth control. And Satan is so good at what he does that most Christians have a hard time even seeing birth control as a problem.

Satan is so good at what he does that most Christians have a hard time even seeing birth control as a problem.

At Compass, we often hear statements similar to this: "What's the problem with planning our lives with fewer kids? Didn't God give us brains?"

Yes, He did give us brains. And with our brains we should be able to discern the difference between God's eternal blessings and earthly temporal blessings.

Most evangelical Christians are horrified at the idea of having 10 or 20 kids. They immediately think of the monetary cost and fatigue factors in raising several children. Using the world's standards, they rule out having as many as God will allow.

But that's from a self-centered, sinful human evaluation. What's missing is asking not what we as sinful humans want but rather what's God's desire for us?

Does God like the idea of us humans cutting back on what He designed? Is artificially reducing the number of kids we have a blessing from the Lord? Or a curse? As you will see, the case will be made that **having fewer kids is a curse in more ways than one.**

Is artificially reducing the number of kids we have a blessing from the Lord?

We've been masterfully duped by the Evil One, buying a lie eerily similar to his lie in the Garden of Eden. Speaking to Eve, Satan said: "You can be God." Eve bought the lie... and so have millions more today.

How Satan duped us....

Let's start with the basics. God says children are a gift, a reward and a blessing from Him.

"Behold, children are a gift of the LORD, the fruit of the womb is a reward." Psa. 127:3

"...his descendants are a blessing." Psa. 37:26

And it's the Lord who blesses us with children:

"...the children whom God has given me." Heb. 2:13

"...I will greatly multiply your descendants so that they will be too many to count." Gen. 16:10

"I will multiply your descendants as the stars of heaven," Gen. 26:4

"May the LORD give you increase, you and your children." Psa. 115:14

"Behold, I and the children whom the LORD has given me ..." Is. 8:18

"the Lord ... opened her womb," Gen. 29:31

"...'shall I ... shut the womb?' says your God." Is. 66:9

I will greatly bless you, and I will greatly multiply your seed as the stars of the heavens.

God even says that a nation's population growth is tied to the defeat of her enemies:

"Indeed I will greatly bless you, and I will greatly multiply your seed as the stars of the heavens and as the sand which is on the seashore; and your seed shall possess the gate of their enemies." Gen. 22:17

"Like arrows in the hand of a warrior, so are the children of one's youth. How blessed is the man whose quiver is full of them; They will not be ashamed when they speak with their enemies in the gate." Psa. 127:4-5

One of the biggest reasons that we should have as many children, as many blessings as God will give us, is that children are *eternal.*

All in this life is temporal and will burn up, *except* the lives of our children. This is amazingly seen in the Book of Job. In chapter 1, Job has:

7,000 sheep
3,000 camels
500 oxen
500 female donkeys
10 children

God allowed all Job had to die, but because of Job's faithfulness, God literally doubled all that Job had lost.

> *"...the Lord restored the fortunes of Job... and ... increased all that Job had twofold." Job 42:10*

But here is the interesting part. Job ended up with:

14,000 sheep
6,000 camels
1,000 oxen
1,000 female donkeys
10 children

How could Job have only received back the same number of children if God doubled them? Why didn't he get back 20 new children?

It's because animals are temporal and children are eternal. Job's first 10 children were still alive in heaven. God counted them as "eternal." When God gave Job 10 more, He *did* double Job's children!

So all this begs the question, "If God wants to bless us, should we *ever* reject His blessings?" Is there ever a Biblical reason not to totally trust the Lord? No, never.

Yet too many Christians do not trust the Lord to give them good gifts all the time. Or they have been duped into believing that they know more than God our Creator. Either way, they just simply don't trust God to do what He says He'll do—make children a blessing.

> ***Trust in the Lord with all your heart and do not lean on your own understanding.***
> ***Proverbs 3:5***

In a nutshell, we want to be in charge, make our own decisions based on what we want...be our own god. So we take the reins of our life and make eternal decisions based on our limited and sinful understanding.

Think of it this way. If Jesus is standing in front of you and says "I want to bless you," will you look Him in the eye and say, "No thanks"? Yet that's what we're doing when we choose fewer children.

Instead of desiring more eternal gifts from God, we are instead desiring more temporal things offered by Satan.

Cars, houses, vacations, lifestyle and more are dangled in front of us like candy. And we take the bait. How could we be happy with a houseful of kids sucking up our cash? We want our stuff!

Worse, we tell God we'll let Him know if or when we change our minds and then expect Him to hop to it and answer our prayers.

So here we are—although God has graciously given us a part in the multiplication of humans in His image, when He chooses to bless us, we are choosing to decline the eternal blessings in favor of having more temporal things in this life.

And consider this...if more children are a blessing, then it's logical that fewer children are a curse.

Ramifications for America

So as a nation, we're choosing to be our own gods and have fewer children. And the ramifications are stark.

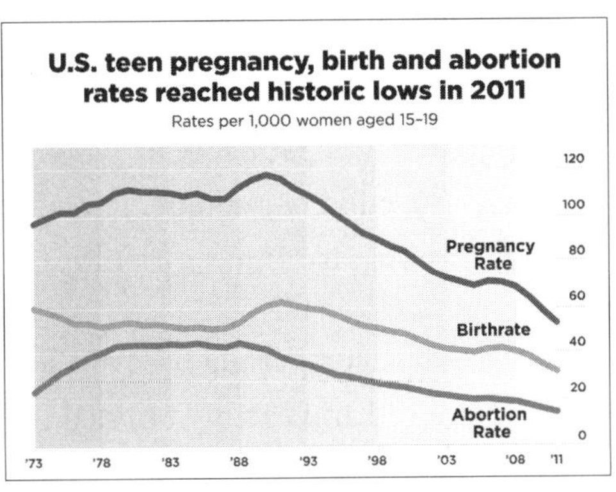

Here are some statistical facts that most Christians never have considered. Consider this first chart...You may have heard that the number of abortions in America is declining. Yes, abortions in America are declining. But as you can clearly see, the lower abortion rate is mainly due to overall pregnancies declining.

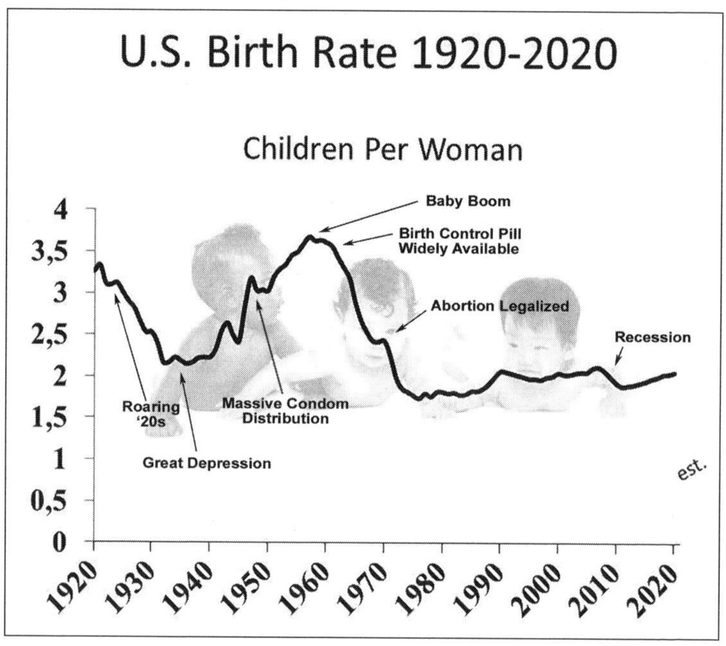

So what changed to make pregnancies decline? Consider the chart at the top of the following page.

To see what happens to our economy, our nation's strength, look at what happens when we use birth control and have one child per couple. In only three generations the eight adults turn into one child.

This is what's happening today in Europe. Europeans are so self-centered and earthly minded that the Muslims, who

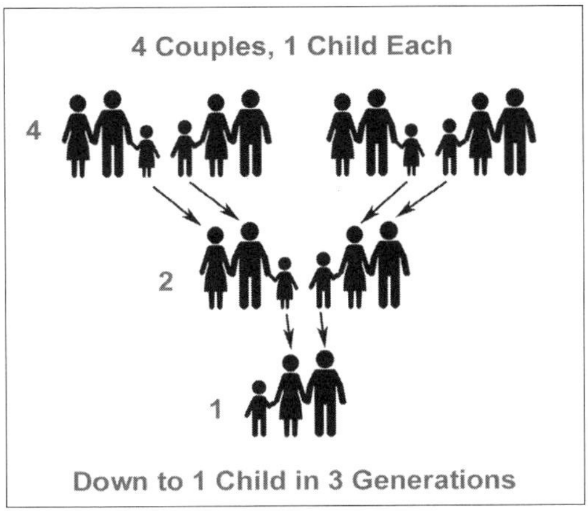

are multiplying like rabbits, will have a majority in only a few years. Europe is being conquered by Islam without firing a shot.

The growth of the Muslim population is well documented. We have to have our heads in the sand not to pay attention to the facts of our enemy's population growth.

Nonie Darwish, founder of Arabs for Israel, said recently that Great Britain has several cities now totally controlled by Muslims. She said, "In twenty years there will be enough Muslims to elect the heads of Government by themselves! Rest assured they will do so."

In Japan, Germany and Italy, the labor pool is actually shrinking! This is also where America is headed. When we have fewer children, our economy shrinks and our strength is sapped. When we soared economically as a nation, we were having six children per couple.

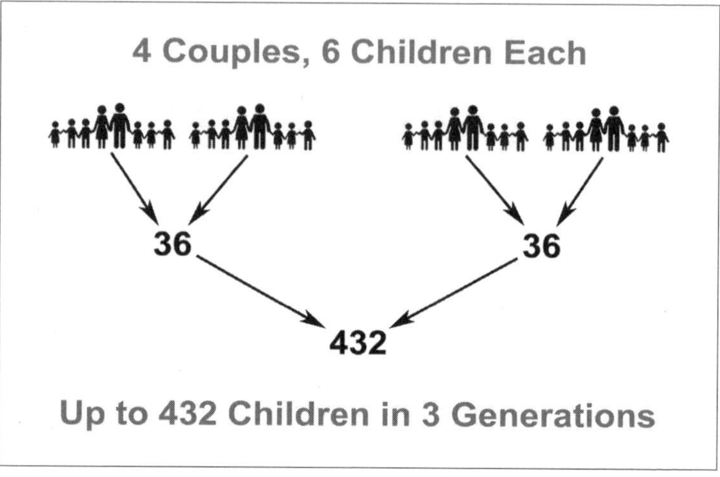

Look what happens when a nation averages six kids per family. In only three generations a family has 432 offspring! That birthrate grew this nation to be the strongest in the world with a humming economy. It was a blessing to have large families.

Today, as a nation, we're averaging two children per couple, which is under the replacement rate. And the white Anglo-Saxon birthrate is down to 1.7. If we were averaging three per couple, instead of two, it would change things drastically.

Even the secular side is picking up on this downtrend in births. A book by Harry Dent, entitled *The Demographic Cliff,* shows a direct correlation between the worldwide declining birthrate and the sputtering economy.

Dent, an economic forecaster, shows that due to the low birthrate in America, there is no way the economy will ever

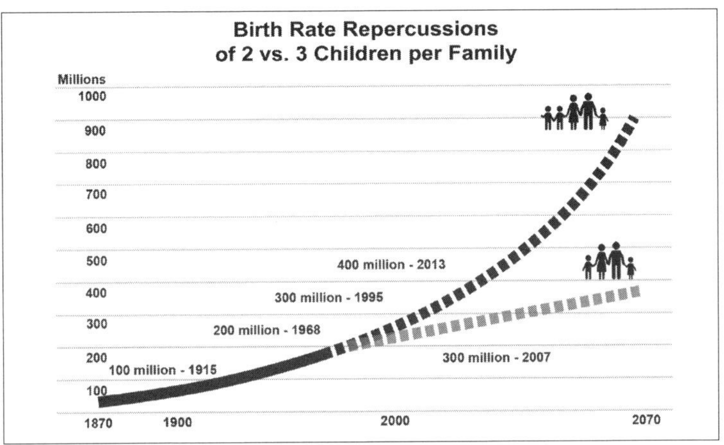

recover to resemble the past.The baby boom, according to Dent, is the last decent economic stimulus left in this country. And as it dies off, so will the economy.

Slower economic growth lowers corporate profits, which limits income and makes it almost impossible for families to raise their living standard. Home prices stagnate or worse.

The bottom line is we're paying a steep price. And this is not even dealing with the *huge* medical issues and problems from using the pill or getting a vasectomy.

So, what's the answer? Obviously for most Christians reading this, it's too late to do anything to have more kids. But we can teach eternal truths to our kids and grandkids. It's never too late to do what's right.

> *"preach the word; be ready in season and out of season; reprove, rebuke, exhort, with great patience and instruction." 2Tim. 4:2*

CHAPTER FIVE

GOD'S PATIENCE IN THE LAST DAYS

I received a phone call recently from a guy who was bound and determined to prove to me that born-again Believers could lose their salvation based on sin.

It didn't matter what I said, how I explained it or what verse I used, he was resolute to stay in his works-oriented doctrinal bondage.

I eventually lost patience and did my best to politely get off the phone with him. But the point is, I lost patience with him. After I hung up, I really got convicted reading this verse:

> *"Therefore I, the prisoner of the Lord, implore you to walk in a manner worthy of the calling with which you have been called, with all humility and gentleness, with patience, showing tolerance for one another in love, being diligent to preserve the unity of the Spirit in the bond of peace." Eph. 4:1-3*

I was not humble with this guy, nor gentle, nor tolerant. I did nothing to preserve Christian unity. And most of all, I was not patient.

The bottom line is that I was in just as much sin losing my patience as he was teaching that Believers can lose their salvation. Licking my wounds, I began looking at what God says about patience.

I remembered that, as new Believers, someone once erroneously taught my wife Susie and me that if we prayed for patience, we would be given many opportunities to practice! It was years before we understood that wasn't true. So I'm extra motivated to be careful in what I learn and teach about patience!

I'm extra motivated to be careful in what I learn and teach about patience!

As often happens in my Bible studies (and I'm sure to many of you too), once I started my study it took a "left turn" in a direction I had never considered. I was surprised to learn that not only is God patient with all of us sinners, we're actually living in a time just before the Rapture that is called "God's patience."

> *"...the patience of God kept waiting in the days of Noah, during the construction of the ark, in which a few, that is, eight persons, were brought safely through the water."*
> *1Pet. 3:20*

I've done a lot of "Days of Noah" comparisons, comparing the days prior to the Flood to today, but somehow I missed this specifically designated time period. But it's quite clear that the time period before Noah's Flood is specifically referred to as a time of "God's patience."

Since Jesus said the time before Rapture will be "just like" the days of Noah, then we are also currently living in the days of God's patience.

The time before Rapture will be "just like" the days of Noah.

Jesus said:

> *"For the coming of the Son of Man will be **just like** the days of Noah." Matt. 24:37*

The Bible says the time before the Flood, when Noah was building the ark, will be "just like" the time before the Rapture when God is building His Church! Therefore, we're currently living in the days of God's patience.

The Bible also says that in the last days before the Rapture, many will "mock" God and His Word, lusting after self and denying that God will return to judge the earth.

Peter said:

> *"Know this first of all, that in the last days mockers will come with their mocking, following after their own lusts,*

and saying, 'Where is the promise of His coming? For ever since the fathers fell asleep, all continues just as it was from the beginning of creation.'" 2Pet. 3:3,4

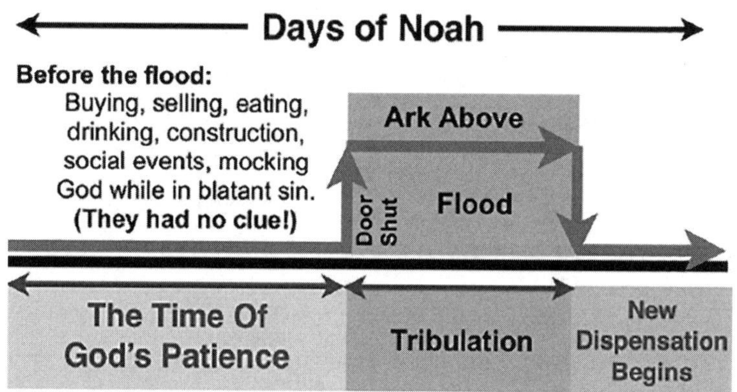

So this chart illustrates what we know about the time prior to the Lord shutting the door on the ark and destroying all living, land-dwelling creatures outside God's protective ark.

And standing out like a sore thumb in the chart above is what Peter calls the "Time of God's Patience."

"...when the <u>patience of God</u> kept waiting in the days of Noah, during the construction of the ark," 1Pet. 3:20

During the hundred-plus years that Noah was building the ark, despite the horrible sin happening all over the earth, God was patient.

God is love and love is patient.

"Love is patient," 1Cor. 13:4

During the time of God's patience before the worldwide Flood, Noah was preaching God's truth. For over one hundred years, while building the ark, Noah warned the people on earth of what was to come.

"[God]*....did not spare the ancient world, but preserved Noah, a preacher of righteousness." 2Pet. 2:5*

Imagine preaching for more than 100 years and no one getting saved! Despite all the sin and corruption for hundreds of years, the Lord was patient during the time the ark was being built.

Noah knew the end was getting close

When Noah and his family finished loading the food and water on the ark and God began to supernaturally bring the animals to load, Noah and his family *knew* the Flood was close. They *knew* the end was near. They could see the writing on the wall! It wasn't rocket science.

They knew that the patience of God was about to end and that He would destroy all wicked mankind on the earth. And, despite Noah's warnings, the wicked were caught totally off-guard.

"As in those days before the flood they were eating and drinking, marrying and giving in marriage, until the day that Noah entered the ark, and they did not under-

stand until the flood came and took them all away; ***so will the coming of the Son of Man be."*** *Matt. 24:38-39*

Therefore, since that is *exactly* how it will be right before the Rapture, then this is how it looks graphically when applied to today:

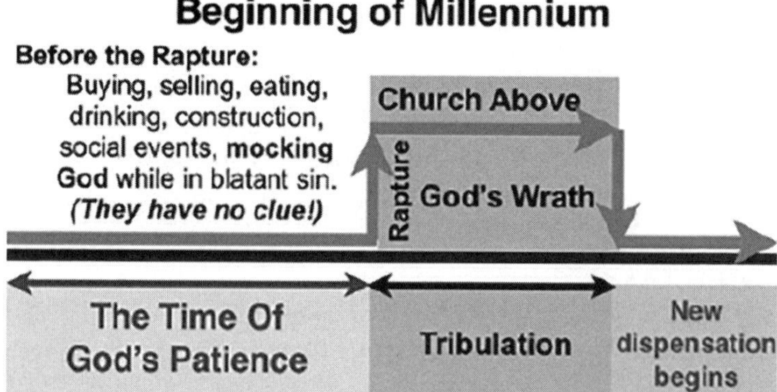

Understanding the time of God's patience explains a lot of things. We really can't fathom God's incomprehensible restraint He's displaying during the time in which we live.

Think about the depths to which we've sunk in the last 50 years without the Lord lowering the boom on those on the earth:

- We've literally murdered some 60 million precious unborn babies in the United States, simply for the sake of convenience. Worldwide, the unfathomable number is over two billion!

"... the LORD hates...an abomination to Him ... hands that shed innocent blood," Prov. 6:16-17

- We've watered down our Biblical armor by not preaching about sin and repentance from our pulpits.

"preach the word; be ready in season and out of season; reprove, rebuke, exhort, with great patience and instruction." 2 Tim. 4:2

- We've made our decisions based on money instead of honor or Biblical principles.

"A good name is to be more desired than great wealth, favor is better than silver and gold." Prov. 22:1

- We've violated the Biblical principle of "no work, no food" calling it "welfare."

"...if anyone is not willing to work, then he is not to eat, either." 2 Thes. 3:10

- We've allowed pornography to infiltrate our homes through television, computers and cell phones. The United States is the world's largest distributor of pornography. Over 50% of our youth admit to having a problem with pornography!

"The eye is the lamp of your body; when your eye is clear, your whole body also is full of light; but when it is bad, your body also is full of darkness." Luke 11:34

- And most recently, our nation has "flipped-the-finger" to our Creator by calling the quite grievous and gruesome sin of homosexuality "normal."

"Woe to those who call evil good, and good evil; who substitute darkness for light and light for darkness;" Is. 5:20

Americans tend to assume God views the United States like He views Israel.

"Woe to those who enact evil statutes and to those who constantly record unjust decisions," Is. 10:1

So why hasn't the Lord judged America, or the earth? The answer is that He will. It's just that currently we're spared because we're in the time period of "God's Patience." But eventually God will lower the boom during the Tribulation time period—the dispensation that follows the Rapture. Consider this carnage to come:

"... every mountain and island were moved out their places..." Rev. 6:14

"... A third of the earth was burned up." Rev. 8:7 (Also, a third of mankind dies, Rev. 9:15)

"... every living thing in the sea died." Rev. 16:3

It's also necessary to note that Americans tend to assume God views the United States like He views Israel, in a special category. But America is not Israel, and we're not in a special category. America has not inherited the promises of Israel.

Yes, as individuals we have been grafted into Israel's promises...

> *"God has not rejected His people whom He foreknew." Rom. 11:2*

> *"For I do not want you, brethren, to be uninformed of this mystery...a partial hardening has happened to Israel until the fullness of the Gentiles has come in; and so all Israel will be saved; just as it is written," Rom. 11:25-26*

Prior to the Church Age, God dealt with Israel as a nation. But today, in the Church Age, God deals with individual Believers.

Yes, as individuals we have been grafted into Israel's promises, but the United States as a country is really no different than any other nation. Believers in other atheistic nations have the same access to the Lord through prayer.

But the rain falls on Believers and non-Believers alike.

> *"... He causes His sun to rise on the evil and the good, and sends rain on the righteous and the unrighteous." Matt. 5:45*

Today, nations can be blessed, or not blessed, based on how they interact with the reborn nation of Israel.

"And I will bless those who bless you [Israel], *and the one who curses you I will curse." Gen. 12:3*

The Lord also says we should pray for our governmental leaders so we can lead a quiet life. So a Believer in Russia has the same situation as we have. We all pray for God's Will to be done.

...there are people He still will draw into the Kingdom and things He wishes to do through Believers before the curtain drops.

*"First of all, then, I urge that entreaties and prayers, petitions and thanksgivings, be made on behalf of all men, for kings and all who are in authority, **so that we may lead a tranquil and quiet life** in all godliness and dignity." 1Tim. 2:1-2*

But the bottom line to us today is that we're in the time of God's Patience. God is withholding what is due for all nations until His plan is perfectly finished. His patience allows for more people to be saved who will avoid the horrors of the Tribulation.

Those who have recently been saved are missing the Tribulation because God has been patiently waiting. Therefore, there are people He still will draw into the Kingdom and things He wishes to do through Believers before the curtain drops with the Rapture. So God tells us to also be "patient!"

"The Lord is not slow about His promise, as some count slowness, but is patient toward you, not wishing for any to perish but for all to come to repentance." 2Pet. 3:9

Those who are saved between now and the Rapture will be rescued because God is patiently waiting for all whom He chose before the foundation of the earth was laid.

"Just as He chose us in Him before the foundation of the world," Eph. 1:4

We don't know if the Lord is coming in the next minute, the next month or years from now. And if the Lord tarries, we have to be patient.

Just like they watched the animals being loaded on the Ark, we too can watch the prophetic signs being fulfilled.

"Therefore be patient, brethren, until the coming of the Lord..." James 5:7

"...regard the patience of our Lord as salvation ..." 2Pet. 3:15

And just like those living in the time of Noah, who saw the animals being loaded on the Ark, we too can see all of the prophecies coming together, lining up exactly as the Bible predicted. Even with people all around us denying it's close!

"And saying, 'Where is the promise of His coming? For ever since the fathers fell asleep, all continues just as it was from the beginning of creation.'" 2Pet. 3:4

So we wait patiently, ready to be used by Him as the days linger on until our great exodus at the Rapture.

> *"So, as those who have been chosen of God, holy and beloved, put on a heart of compassion, kindness, humility, gentleness and patience;" Col. 3:12*

In the parable of the Nobleman (Luke 19:12-27) there is an inference to "occupy" or "stay busy" until the Lord returns. So we wait patiently, staying busy with our duties while praying that He will use us to witness to someone in our family, a neighbor, or someone at work, someone who still needs to get in on the Church exit.

So this is one incredible time in which we, as Believers, should be very sensitive to God's leading. There is one person on the planet who will be the last person saved prior to our removal.

Much like the thief on the cross, one person will be the last to believe. That person will be the last to receive God's gift of the Holy Spirit

Much like the thief on the cross, one person will be the last to believe. That person will be the last to receive God's gift of the Holy Spirit, being permanently indwelled by Him. He or she will be whisked away with the rest of the Believers, escaping God's horrific judgment coming on earth.

But until that departure day, we can have peace in God's latter-days patience, knowing that despite what we see all around us, *the Lord is still in control.* Nothing is happening that He's not allowing.

And when it's all over, we win. So let's live like we know we've already won!

CHAPTER SIX

WHEN BELIEVERS DIE

"... the day of one's death is better than the day of one's birth." Eccl. 7:1

Death is one thing all humans have in common. Roughly 150,000 people die every day, about 107 per minute. Most of us have had close family or friends die. Let's face it, we're all basically dying—some sooner than others.

Here at Compass we're often contacted by people who have a terminal illness and are looking for Biblical information on what happens when Believers die. So this chapter is meant to be a succinct tour of the key verses dealing with a Believer transitioning from earth to heaven.

Death Is Certain

Only Enoch escaped earthly death (Gen 5:24). Elijah was taken up in the fiery chariot (2 Kings 2:11), but he will return and die as one of the two witnesses in the Tribulation

(Mal. 4:5). I believe and teach that John has yet to die (John 21:20-23), but he will eventually die in the Tribulation as the other witness (Rev. 11:3, 7). [Compass has an article titled "The Identity of the Two Witnesses" at compass.org.]

So chances are, with the obvious exception of the timing of the Rapture, one day you're going to die. So what happens when you die? The Bible gives us some fascinating insight into what happens next.

Luke 16:19-31 records an actual event—not a parable—about two people dying, prior to the Cross. One man dies and goes to Paradise, the place where Believers went who died waiting for the Messiah to pay for their sins so they could go to heaven. He had a body, was fully conscious and was in comfort.

So what happens when you die? The Bible gives us some fascinating insight into what happens next.

The other man went to Hades. There he also had a body, was fully conscious, and could think, reason, speak and feel pain. His words are chilling.

> *"In Hades he lifted up his eyes, being in torment, and saw Abraham far away and Lazarus in his bosom. And he cried out and said, 'Father Abraham, have mercy on me, and send Lazarus so that he may dip the tip of his finger in water and cool off my tongue, for I am in agony in this flame.'" Luke 16:23-24*

Thankfully, for those of us who are born again in the Church Age, who are Believers trusting in the Gospel, the Good News of Jesus' death and resurrection, our sins are not counted against us and we will one day go straight to heaven when we die.

Before we die, we live our lives as aliens on a planet that was hijacked by Satan.

"... having forgiven us ***all*** *our transgressions, having canceled out the certificate of debt consisting of decrees against us, which was hostile to us; and He has taken it out of the way, having nailed it to the cross." Col. 2:13b-14*

"I prefer to be absent from the body and be at home with the Lord." 2Cor 5:8

Heaven Will Knock Your Socks Off!

The Bible says heaven is better than we can imagine.

"But just as it is written, 'Things which eye has not seen and ear has not heard, and which have not entered the heart of man, all that God has prepared for those who love Him.'" 1Cor. 2:9

I have quite an imagination. Yet regardless of what I can imagine would be wonderfully incredible in heaven, it's better than that! But before we die, we live our lives as aliens on a planet that was hijacked by Satan. Satan is "the god of this world" (2 Cor 4:4) and he's hostile to Believers.

So Believers live in this life looking forward to the next.

"For our citizenship is in heaven, from which also we eagerly wait for a Savior, the Lord Jesus Christ;" Phil. 3:20

The very brief time between our birth and death is referred to simply as a "vapor."

"You are just a vapor that appears for a little while and then vanishes away." James 4:14b

Because of all of Satan's evil influence in the world, we tend to define our life span in terms of what's taking place in our life that's bad...

In our time on earth God allows us to have many blessings, but no one is blessed with all good or cursed with all bad. Sometimes we experience periods of absolute joy; other times are difficult and painful.

But by keeping our eyes up, on our eternal destiny, we're thankful for the good times while enduring the bad.

"Set your mind on the things above, not on the things that are on earth." Col. 3:2

We're grateful for any good times in our earthly life because the Lord gives them. If it were up to Satan, our entire lives would all be nothing but horror and despair.

Death Removes Evil

Because of Satan's evil influence in the world, we tend to define our lifespan in terms of what's taking place in our life that's bad... i.e., weather disasters, tidal waves, earthquakes, wars, sickness, divorce, etc.

Most Believers don't think in terms of death as being good.

But realistically, our life span should be defined by God's blessings—things which we don't deserve but are graciously given by God like our birth, salvation and children. And of all God has given us, **the cherry on the top of life's cake is death.**

Most Believers don't think in terms of death as being good. Yet for Believers, death is God's way of removing all evil and sickness from our lives.

After Adam and Eve sinned, God prevented them from eating from the tree of life because had they eaten from it, the whole human race would have lived forever in that horrible, sinful condition.

> *"Then the LORD God said, "Behold, the man has become like one of Us, knowing good and evil; and now, he might stretch out his hand, and take also from the tree of life, and eat, and live forever" Gen. 3:22*

> *"So He drove the man out; and at the east of the garden of Eden He stationed the cherubim and the flaming*

sword which turned every direction to guard the way to the tree of life." Gen. 3:24

God allowed death in order that we could be redeemed. God even speaks of a Believer's transition to the next life by chiding death.

"O Death, where is your victory? O Death, where is your sting?" 1 Cor. 15:55

God Says Death Is A Positive

Remarkably, God refers to death in glowing terms.

"Precious in the sight of the LORD is the death of His godly ones." Psa. 116:15

In Paul's second letter to the Corinthians, he describes being taken to heaven, briefly seeing the next life, and was never the same again. He badly wanted to return to heaven but set an example for us by being content to live within God's divine plan (2 Cor 12:2-10).

In his very next letter, Paul writes to the Christians in Rome and says:

"Wretched man that I am! Who will set me free from the body of this death?" Rom. 7:24

Later Paul writes to the Christians in Philippi that he was torn between desiring to die and staying on earth.

> *"But if I am to live on in the flesh, this will mean fruitful labor for me; and I do not know which to choose. But I am hard-pressed from both directions, having the desire to depart and be with Christ, for that is very much better; yet to remain on in the flesh is more necessary for your sake." Phil. 1:22-24*

To the Christians in Corinth he said he would rather be dead because he would immediately be with the Lord.

> *"Therefore, being always of good courage, and knowing that while we are at home in the body we are absent from the Lord. ...I say, and prefer rather to be absent from the body and to be at home with the Lord." 2Cor. 5:6,8*

For this perishable must put on the imperishable, and this mortal must put on immortality.

Death Is A Victory

Paul even refers to death as a "victory."

> *"For this perishable must put on the imperishable, and this mortal must put on immortality. But when this perishable will have put on the imperishable, and this mortal will have put on immortality, then will come about the saying that is written, 'Death is swallowed up in victory.'" 1 Cor 15:53-54*

Do you fear death? Jesus says His death rendered powerless the devil so you can live confidently in this life without that fear.

> *"...through death He might render powerless him who had the power of death, that is, the devil, and might free those who through fear of death were subject to slavery all their lives." Heb. 2:14-15*

So death is an *upgrade* for Believers. It's something to anticipate with great eagerness because it is at that moment we win! In one instant, we go from this sinful earth to heavenly glory.

> *"I will dwell in the house of the LORD forever." Ps. 23:6b*

So realistically, God says death for Believers is not something to fear but for which to be grateful—grateful to be rid of this sinful body, no longer dealing with the lust of the eyes, lust of the flesh and the pride of life.

When we die, we discard our temporal earthly container and receive a new eternal container...

Receiving Our New Container

When we die, we discard our temporal earthly container and receive a new eternal container to house our spirit, the only thing that's worth saving. Paul puts it this way:

> *"For we know that if the earthly tent which is our house is torn down, we have a building from God, a house not made with hands, eternal in the heavens. For indeed in this house we groan, longing to be clothed with our dwelling from heaven," 2 Cor. 5:1-2*

And this new eternal container, built by God to house our spirit, will look just like Jesus' body after the resurrection.

> *"...the Lord Jesus Christ; who will transform the body of our humble state into conformity with the body of His glory..." Phil. 3:20b-21*

After the resurrection Jesus walked around, ate and drank. Our new body will be like His resurrected body—flesh and bone.

> *"See My hands and My feet, that it is I Myself; touch Me and see, for a spirit does not have flesh and bones as you see that I have." Luke 24:39*

Therefore we'll be given a new body that has arms, legs, eyes, etc., and will be recognizable to others but without being subject to the debilitating physical effects that sin brings.

More amazingly, we will be able to move at the speed of thought, as Jesus appeared and disappeared at will. He also walked through walls. We will be able to do the same. With our new body we will be able to eat and drink, as Jesus did after His resurrection.

> *"Truly I say to you, I will never again drink of the fruit of the vine until that day when I drink it new in the kingdom of God." Mark 14:25*

All Believers who have been handicapped in this life will no longer be restricted. Those confined to beds in this life will have perfect and complete freedom of movement...and without pain.

Those blind on this earth will be given perfect eternal eyes to see. And no diseases will ever affect us again. No heartbreak of any kind will penetrate our existence.

> *"And He will wipe away every tear from their eyes; and there will no longer be any death; there will no longer be any mourning, or crying, or pain; the first things have passed away." Rev. 21:4*

Those who are suffering from disease are immediately healed... death is the ultimate form of healing! And we'll labor no more, no more toiling for sustenance.

Believers Don't Die

Believers don't really die, in the sense of being dead or ceasing to exist. When we leave this earth, we'll be more alive than ever before.

When we take our last breath, we immediately go to be with the Lord. No waiting. No trial. No evaluation. No judgment. Jesus paid it all so when we die we go to be with Him.

> *"Therefore there is now no condemnation for those who are in Christ Jesus." Rom. 8:1*

John's Gospel says this incredible position of "no condemnation" is attained when we first believe the Gospel.

> *"Truly, truly, I say to you, he who hears My word, and believes Him who sent Me, has eternal life, and does not come into judgment, but has passed out of death into life." John 5:24*

God Determines When We Die

It is also noteworthy that our number of days on this planet is determined by God *prior* to our being born.

> *"Your eyes have seen my unformed substance; and in Your book were all written The days that were ordained for me, When as yet there was not one of them." Psa. 139:16*

If dying is gain, shouldn't Believers look forward to this transition?

> *"There is an appointed time for everything. And there is a time for every event under heaven - A time to give birth and a time to die;" Eccl. 3:1-2*

God also tells us that worrying about death is fruitless.

> *"And which of you by worrying can add a single hour to his life's span?" Luke 12:25*

So God determines how long we'll live. But that doesn't mean we throw caution to the wind and play in traffic. We don't put the Lord to a foolish test. Rather, we live for Him and know when we die it's even better.

"For to me, to live is Christ and to die is gain." Phil. 1:21

So we can live boldly in this life, knowing God is in control.

If dying is gain, shouldn't Believers look forward to this transition? God says to wait eagerly for our body to be redeemed!

"...waiting eagerly for our adoption as sons, the redemption of our body." Rom. 8:23b

Death for Believers should be thought of in the highest and most secure terms. We have paradise waiting for us!

"Blessed be the God and Father of our Lord Jesus Christ, who according to His great mercy has caused us to be born again to a living hope through the resurrection of Jesus Christ from the dead, to obtain an inheritance which is imperishable and undefiled and will not fade away, ***reserved in heaven for you,****" 1Pet. 1:3-4*

So our spot is "reserved," and we're waiting on God's timing for our transition.

"Jesus said to her, 'I am the resurrection and the life; he who believes in Me will live even if he dies, and everyone who lives and believes in Me will never die.'" John 11:25-26

So we can live boldly in this life, knowing God is in control of our death and destiny. Even if we see death approaching, we're comforted by what God promises will follow.

> *"Even though I walk through the valley of the shadow of death, I fear no evil, for You are with me; Your rod and Your staff, they comfort me." Psa. 23:4*

The Possibility of Rapture

There is a possibility, maybe a good one, that you're living in the day of the great Believer exodus called the Rapture. The two main verses discussing the Rapture are:

> ***The Rapture is a necessity because Believers are not appointed to God's wrath.***

> *"Behold, I tell you a mystery; we will not all sleep, but we will all be changed, in a moment, in the twinkling of an eye, at the last trumpet; for the trumpet will sound, and the dead will be raised imperishable, and we will be changed. For this perishable must put on the imperishable, and this mortal must put on immortality." 1Cor. 15:51-53*

> *"For this we say to you by the word of the Lord, that we who are alive and remain until the coming of the Lord, will not precede those who have fallen asleep. For the Lord Himself will descend from heaven with a shout, with the voice of the archangel and with the trumpet of God, and the dead in Christ will rise first. Then we who*

are alive and remain will be caught up together with them in the clouds to meet the Lord in the air, and so we shall always be with the Lord." 1Thes. 4:15-17

The Rapture is a necessity because Believers are not appointed to God's wrath.

For God has not destined us for wrath, but for obtaining salvation...

"For God has not destined us for wrath, but for obtaining salvation through our Lord Jesus Christ," 1Thes. 5:9

"... Jesus, who rescues us from the wrath to come." 1Thes. 1:10b

"Much more then, having now been justified by His blood, we shall be saved from the wrath of God through Him." Rom. 5:9

Therefore, Christians who are alive at the end of the Church Age will be translated, caught up in the air, to meet Jesus. This removal of Believers from the earth paves the way for the seven-year Tribulation, when God's wrath will be poured out on those who are left on earth.

"...the wrath of God..." Rev. 15:1

"...seven golden bowls full of the wrath of God," Rev. 15:7

"...seven bowls of the wrath of God." Rev. 16:1

"...the wine of His fierce wrath." Rev. 16:19

If you're a Believer who is alive the moment God ends the Church Age, you will participate in the Rapture, a quite spine-tingling event! You won't die a natural death, but the result will be the same—you will immediately disappear from the earth and be with the Lord Jesus, forever.

So knowing what's ahead for Believers in the future, due to death or Rapture, how then should we live? We live looking up, not down. The Bible sums it up this way:

> *"For not one of us lives for himself, and not one dies for himself; for if we live, we live for the Lord, or if we die, we die for the Lord; therefore whether we live or die, we are the Lord's." Rom. 14:7-8*

So look forward to your transition to the next life—we win!

CHAPTER SEVEN

AMERICA IN BIBLE PROPHECY

Most Bible prophecy teachers teach that the United States is not in Bible prophecy. I disagree. I believe the United States is mentioned specifically, scores of times, and is described in great detail.

I know I will receive a lot of mail on this, so my only request is that before you tell me that I am wrong, first tell me who this nation could possibly be... other than the United States!

The words "United States" or "America" are not in Scripture. But often buried within Scriptural text is a parallel revelation or dual fulfillment.

Obvious examples of this double reference are in Isaiah 14 and Ezekiel 28. In Isaiah 14:4, the text begins with references to the "king of Babylon," but gradually changes into comments about Satan:

"How you have fallen from heaven..." Is. 14:12

The same is true with Ezekiel 28, where verse 11 speaks of the "king of Tyre," but verse 13 moves into specific traits and characteristics of Satan: "...you were in the garden of God." It's from these two chapters that many of Satan's characteristics are revealed, yet we had to dig a little first before we could uncover the Scriptural jewels buried therein.

"It is the glory of God to conceal a matter..." Prov. 25:2

If we are living in the final decades, years or days of the Church Age, America, still the #1 power in the world, could logically be in the Bible somewhere. Applying the above principle of "Double Reference," or "Duel Fulfillment," there are numerous verses in the Bible that may give us some insight into what ultimately happens to America in the future.

Below is a list of the characteristics of an end-time, latter-day nation. I'll challenge you to find another country, other than the United States, that fully fits this description!

Who Is This Nation?

The Bible calls this unnamed nation "Babylon" and sometimes refers to it as the "Daughter of Babylon." Most of the following characteristics of Babylon are taken from verses in Jeremiah 50, 51, Isaiah 18, 47 and Revelation 17, 18.

These Scriptures record a fascinating description of a nation that has much wisdom, wealth and knowledge, thinks it is secure and invincible, but is suddenly totally destroyed.

Bordered By Many Waters

"O you who dwell by many waters..." Jer 51:13

"The sea has come up over Babylon; She has been engulfed with its tumultuous waves." Jer 51:42

This is a nation that is bordered by "many waters." Later you will see that it also imports primarily by ships. It is important to note that Babylon in Iraq has two relatively small ports on only one ocean. In comparison, America is virtually surrounded by water. It has no fewer than 15 major ports, on three oceans, five Great Lakes and the Mississippi River.

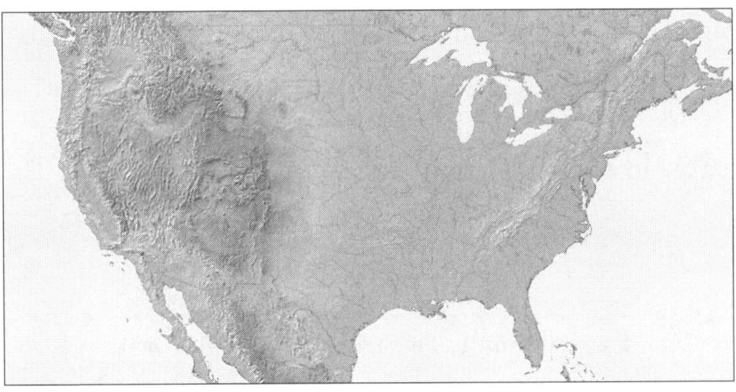

Has A Mother Nation

"Your mother will be greatly ashamed, she who gave you birth will be humiliated. Behold, she will be the [youngest] *of the nations..." Jer 50:12*

This nation has a mother nation . . . like America has a mother nation—Great Britain. And this nation is the youngest of the world's superpowers at the end of the Church Age.

Militarily Strong

"How the hammer of the whole earth has been cut off and broken!..." Jer. 50:23

He says, "You are My war-club, My weapon of war;" Jer. 51:20a

This nation is the military hammer of the earth. We have military troops deployed in more than 150 countries around the world, with over 300,000 of our active-duty personnel serving outside the United States and its territories. No one else comes close to this world-wide military dominance.

Large Importing Nation

"Come to her from the farthest border; open up her barns," Jer. 50:26a

"And the merchants of the earth weep and mourn over her, because no one buys their cargoes any more..." Rev. 18:11

"...the merchants of the earth have become rich by the wealth of her..." Rev. 18:3b

The United States is the largest single importing nation in the world.

A Wealthy Nation

"....such great wealth..." Rev. 18:17

"Babylon has been a golden cup in the hand of the LORD, intoxicating all the earth." Jer. 51:7

This nation is agriculturally abundant, wealthy, has world-wide influence and is a large importing nation via the sea.

And the merchants of the earth weep and mourn over her, because no one buys their cargoes any more...

An Educated Nation

"A sword against . . . her wise men!" Jer 50:35

This nation is very educated. The United States has historically been either the top or one of the top nations in the world regarding educating her population. From putting a man on the moon to building great bridges and dams, America has been blessed with wise men.

Population Diversity

"A sword against... all the foreigners who are in the midst of her," Jer. 50:37a

This nation is full of foreigners, legal and/or illegal. The *King James Version* calls it a "Mingled-People Nation." The U.S. is about as "mingled" as a nation can get!

Abundant in Natural Resources

"...A sword against her treasures, . . ." Jer. 50:37b

"Abundant in treasures, . . ." Jer. 51:13

This nation had been blessed by God. Use any measurement you wish—the United States is quite abundant in natural resources. Coal, oil, forests, gold, silver, energy from rivers... the list is endless.

A Nation Full of Idols

". . . Her images have been put to shame, her idols have been shattered." Jer. 50:2d

". . . it is the land of idols, and they are mad over fearsome idols." Jer. 50:38

This nation had been blessed by God. Use any measurement you wish—the United States is quite abundant.

The nation in question has a lot of "images." How would Isaiah describe TV, movies, or the Internet 3000 years ago? And, any way you define "idol," the United States is full of them. An idol is anything that you put before God.

Money, cars, sex, TV, football, pornography, self, etc., would certainly qualify as "idols." Amazingly, one of the top TV shows in the United States was named *American Idol,* and we have a national magazine titled *SELF*. If the shoe fits...

Space Program?

"Though Babylon should ascend to the heavens." Jer. 51:53

If that is a reference to this nation taking space shots, it certainly narrows the field of prospective countries that could qualify! Since 1958, NASA has led the world in space exploration through its Apollo moon landings, Skylab and Space Shuttles.

Has Become Arrogant

"... For she has become arrogant against the LORD, against the Holy One of Israel." Jer. 50:29c

"Behold, I am against you, O arrogant one," declares the Lord GOD of hosts, for your day has come, the time when I will punish you." Jer. 50:31

This nation "has become arrogant against the Lord," indicating that at one time the nation was once humble before the Lord. Not just arrogant against God, but specifically arrogant against Jesus Christ, the "Holy One of Israel."

Maybe killing 60 million innocent babies through abortion, being the pornography distribution center of the world, and taking God out of the classroom has something to do with it.

Daughter of Babylon

"... Against you, O daughter of Babylon." Jer. 50:42c

This nation is also referred to as the "daughter" of Babylon. Not the original Babylon, but another country.

Attacked from the North

"...a nation has come up against her out of the north;" Jer. 50:3a

"For the destroyers will come to her from the north..." Jer. 51:48b

The nation is attacked from the north. Interestingly, Russia (Gog) is aligned with Iran (Persia) in the Ezekiel 38-39 post-Rapture invasion of Israel. If the U.S. did receive a nuclear attack from Russia, it would come against the United States over the North Pole, "from the north."

This "shout" might be a reference to the Rapture (1Thes. 4:16), indicating it is still a future event.

The U.S. could be the "coastlands" (Ezek. 39:6) who also get attacked in the Gog invasion.

Rapture Related?

"At the shout, 'Babylon has been seized!' the earth is shaken, and an outcry is heard among the nations." Jer. 50:46

This "shout" might be a reference to the Rapture (1Thes. 4:16), indicating it is still a future event. The earth will definitely be shaken at the Rapture. Or the "shaking" might be America in the seventh bowl of wrath.

"...Babylon the Great was remembered before God, to give her the cup of wine of His fierce wrath. And every island fled away, and the mountains were not found." Rev. 16:19-20

Luxury, Culture and Industry

"The fruit you long for has gone from you, and all things that were luxurious and splendid have passed away from you and men will no longer find them." Rev. 18:14

"And the sound of harpists and musicians and flute-players and trumpeters will not be heard in you any longer; and no craftsman of any craft will be found in you any longer; and the sound of a mill will not be heard in you any longer;" Rev. 18:22

This nation lives in luxury and splendor with many musicians, craftsmen, mills and factories. It is quite an advanced nation, allowed by God Himself.

Worldwide Merchants

"...your merchants were the great men of the earth..." Rev. 18:23

This nation reaches the far corners of the earth with her dominating trade. The United States certainly qualifies with its hundreds of multinational corporations such as IBM, Exxon, Apple, Johnson and Johnson, Microsoft, Coke, McDonalds, etc.

Destruction Happens Without Warning

"Suddenly Babylon has fallen and been broken;" Jer. 51:8a

"...for in one hour such great wealth has been laid waste!" Rev. 18:17a

"...these two things shall come on you suddenly in one day..." Is. 47:9a

"...destruction about which you do not know will come on you suddenly." Is. 47:11c

"Suddenly" could be another reference to the Rapture or possibly a post-Rapture nuclear attack that takes out this nation. The phrase "in one hour" could also be translated "in a moment." The Greek word used there, *hora,* was translated "moment" in two other places in the Bible. So it too could be a reference to the Rapture.

Has Good And Evil

"For thus says the LORD of hosts, the God of Israel: "The daughter of Babylon is like a threshing floor at the time it is stamped firm; Yet in a little while the time of harvest will come for her." Jer. 51:33

This nation is compared to a "threshing floor." It is a nation that for the moment has both good and bad people, but eventually God promises to come get the good —those cleansed by Jesus' blood—at the Rapture.

Lots of Whirring

"Alas, oh land of whirring wings..." Is. 18:1

This nation has a lot of "whirring" going on. Airplanes, helicopters, and other engines make a whirring sound.

Sends Diplomats Worldwide

"Which sends envoys by the sea, Even in papyrus vessels on the surface of the waters. Go, swift messengers, to a nation tall and smooth, To a people feared far and wide, A powerful and oppressive nation whose land the rivers divide." Is. 18:2

This end-time nation sends diplomats around the world, is considered "tall and smooth," is known worldwide, and has plenty of water due to many rivers dividing the land.

This nation, whoever it is, is wiped out in one hour, either by the Rapture or a nuclear attack sometime after the Rapture.

So, for those that insist that Babylon *must* be rebuilt in Iraq to fulfill Bible prophecy, I submit Iraq doesn't fit the above Scriptures. Iraq is not bordered on many waters, it is not the world's military hammer, it is not full of wise men, it is not a mingled-people nation, it is not the world's largest importer, it is not a new or young nation, it does not have plenty of water, and it certainly doesn't take space shots!

This nation, whoever it is, is wiped out in one hour, either by the Rapture or a nuclear attack sometime after the Rapture. Could this be America? With the Church gone and nothing but liberal non-Believers left, in God's perfect timing, it sure seems to fit!

But in the meantime, God bless America!

CHAPTER EIGHT

IS THE RAPTURE IN SEPTEMBER?

We believe that the Rapture will probably be in September, regardless of the year. Here's why!

According to Leviticus 23, there are seven Jewish Feasts commanded by God to be observed each year.

Feast Name	Date	In Hebrew
Passover	Nisan 14 (Apr/May)	Pesach
Unleavened Bread	Nisan 15	Hag Ha Matzot
Firstfruits	Day after Sabbath after Passover	Bikkurim
Feast of Weeks	50 Days after Firstfruits	Shavuot
Trumpets	Tishri 1 (Sep/Oct)	Rosh HaShanah
Day of Atonement	Tishri 10	Yom Kippur
Tabernacles	Tishri 15	Succoth

The symbolism of Jesus in the Jewish Feast of Passover has been extensively analyzed by numerous scholars. In a nutshell, Jesus is our Passover Lamb, the Lamb of God.

"...Christ our Passover..." 1 Cor. 5:7

Shavuot

Jesus was slain on the Cross on Mt. Moriah. At the same time, the Jews were slaying their Passover lambs (it had to be a male lamb without blemish), also on Mt. Moriah, just a few steps away.

There is also symbolism in the other feasts as well.

The Second Feast

The Feast of Unleavened Bread is the day after Passover. Jewish days began at 6 p.m., so this feast began in the evening after Passover.

"...Behold, the Lamb of God who takes away the sin of the world!" John 1:29

Leaven in the Bible is a symbol of sin. The Jews purged their houses of leaven, in conjunction with what the sacrificial lamb had done—removed sin. This is a picture of what Jesus had done on the Cross.

"I am the Bread of life." John 6:48

Feast of Firstfruits

This was to be celebrated on the Sunday after the Sabbath following Passover.

"But now Christ has been raised from the dead,
the first fruits of those who are asleep." 1Cor. 15:20

They celebrated Firstfruits by offering a sheaf of grain to the Lord for His allowing the first harvest.

Jesus is called the "first fruits" from the dead.

Feast of Weeks

Fifty days after Firstfruits, the Jews celebrated the Feast of Weeks. Here the Jews offered two loaves of bread, as a second offering to the Lord, but this time they were baked with leaven, which again symbolizes sin.

While the Jews were celebrating the Feast of Weeks, the Holy Spirit came roaring to earth.

"Wretched man that I am!" Rom. 7:24a

The two loaves could represent either the Old and New Testament, the wheat and the tares, or the Jews and Gentiles being included in the New Testament Church. The leaven represents sin's existence in the Church. That's an understatement!

While the Jews were celebrating the Feast of Weeks, the Holy Spirit came roaring to earth, filling them (Acts 2) at what Christians call "Pentecost."

The symbolism of Jesus and the Church in the first four spring Jewish feasts is undeniable. Think about it, the first four major events of the Church Age—Jesus' death, burial, resurrection, and the coming of the Holy Spirit—all fell exactly on the days of the Jewish Feasts!

But there is a break between the spring and fall feasts.The break in the feasts may very well represent the break in God's plan for the Jews... the Church Age.

If God had the first four major events of the Church Age land exactly on the Jewish Feast days, it is almost a given that the next big Church Age event, the Rapture, will land on the next Jewish Feast in the fall.... whichever year Rapture takes place.

Rosh Hashannah

The next feast in order falls in September or October each year. Called Rosh Hashanah, it's a day of gathering and celebration, and the Jews are specifically charged to "blow trumpets." The blowing of a ram's horn was the signal that it was time to gather in Jerusalem.

For this feast, the Jews would blow the shofar 99 times. This was followed by *Tekiah Gedolah,* "The Great Blowing," which was one last, long blast of the trumpet.

"Now in the seventh month, on the first day of the month, you shall also have a holy convocation; you shall do no la-

borious work. It will be to you a day for blowing trumpets."
Num. 29:1

As all who have studied the Rapture know, the Rapture is a day of gathering in the air and should be quite the celebration! The two most famous spine-tingling Rapture verses read:

> *"In a moment, in the twinkling of an eye,* ***at the last trumpet****; for the trumpet will sound, and the dead will be raised imperishable, and we will be changed."*
> *1Cor. 15:52*

> *"For the Lord Himself will descend from heaven with a shout, with the voice of the archangel and with the* ***trumpet of God****, and the dead in Christ will rise first."*
> *1Thes. 4:16*

Therefore, following God's pattern of having the first four major events of the Church Age land on the first four Jewish feasts, we think the next big event of the Church Age is likely to occur on Rosh Hashanah, regardless of the year! Is that cool or what!

CHAPTER NINE

THE PRE-WRATH DECEPTION

"Whenever he speaks a lie, he speaks from his own nature, for he is a liar and the father of lies." John 8:44b

I get letters and phone calls...

One of the few downsides to working in the ministry here at Compass is that pretty much weekly I have someone new trying to convince me that the Rapture will somehow *not* happen at the end of the Church Age, but rather, happen sometime during the seven-year Tribulation period.

I get phone calls, letters, charts, tapes, books and videos all arguing the mid-trib, post-trib or pre-wrath positions. These impassioned people are usually so convinced their position is correct, and my position is wrong, they think I should spend hours on end listening to and debating them.

For the record, I think the books on the pre-wrath Rapture of the Church have caused the Body of Christ a great deal of pain and confusion. I think these authors mean well, but the books promote, in my opinion, pure heresy.

I feel badly for people deceived by this teaching because I too was once deceived into believing the pre-wrath argument. When I was a new Believer in the 1970s, I was taught by my well-meaning pastor that "mid-trib" Rapture was a fact, not a theory. He gave all the same arguments I hear today, usually centered in some shape, form or fashion around these **two incorrect premises:**

1) We're Saved Only from God's Wrath

Pre-wrathers believe that "God's Wrath" comes only in the last 3 1/2 years of the tribulation—erroneously believing that the first 3 1/2 years are not actually "God's Wrath."

That is, of course, ridiculous! The entire seven-year tribulation period is called "The time of Jacob's Trouble." Good grief, in the first 3 1/2 years there's world-wide economic collapse, famine and one-fourth of the earth dies... sure sounds like "God's Wrath" to me!

2) We Need to Prepare for the Inevitable

Pre-wrathers believe they should plan for the worst-case scenario because if they're wrong, they conclude it won't matter. But if they're right, they'll be prepared.

This is a horrible way to live. Instead of living boldly for the Lord, looking forward to His coming to take us to heaven, the pre-wrathers worry about the Antichrist coming!

But, in fact, if you live to see the Antichrist, you've missed the Rapture!

He who now restrains will do so until he is taken out of the way.

> *"And you know what restrains him now, so that in his time he will be revealed. For the mystery of lawlessness is already at work; only He who now restrains* [the Holy Spirit] *will do so until he is taken out of the way* [via the Rapture]. *Then that lawless one will be revealed..." 2Thes. 2:6-8*

One of the cornerstones of Bible prophecy doctrine is that we're to keep our eyes looking up to heaven, to our future home, not down on this earth. We are to look for Jesus, not the Antichrist!

> *"Set your mind on the things above, not on the things that are on earth." Col. 3:2*

I eventually moved on from my first church, which also tended to border on legalism—common among pre-wrathers. And as I continued to read my Bible through the years, the more I could not Scripturally defend the mid-trib position, or its close cousin, pre-wrath.

Noah Knows

We've shown earlier in this book that the Bible declares the time before the Rapture would be "just like" the days before Noah's Flood. "Just like"! And then Scripture lists the characteristics of that day that our day will be "just like." It couldn't be any clearer.

> *"For the coming of the Son of Man will be just like the days of Noah. For as in those days before the flood they were eating and drinking, marrying and giving in marriage, until the day that Noah entered the ark, and they did not understand until the flood came and took them all away; so will the coming of the Son of Man be." Matt. 24:37-39*

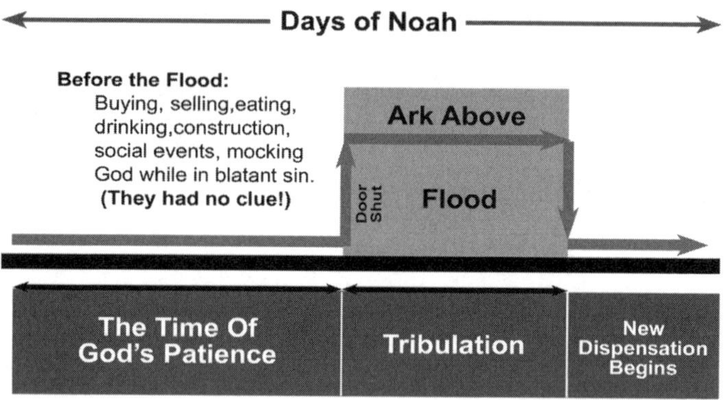

Before the Flood it was "business as usual" with parties, food, building... until God shut the door, which is the symbolic equivalent of the Rapture. This Biblical truth has to be patently ignored by those holding to a pre-wrath position.

To accept pre-wrath you have to say the first 3 1/2 years of the 70th Week of Daniel are no different than today. Really?

In the first 3 1/2 years of Tribulation, Revelation 6 says the earth is in chaos, the worldwide economy collapses, and inflation is so rampant it takes a day's wage just to buy food. Not to mention all this causes 1/4 of the earth to die from war and wild beasts! Does that sound like Jesus' description of the Days of Noah? Hardly!

The Inerrant Word of God

The biggest problem with anything but pre-tribulational Rapture is that you have to abandon using Biblical Dispensations to interpret Scripture. This is the purest of all doctrines because it's rooted in using a literal hermeneutic to interpret Scripture.

It seems like every day we get an email or call from someone who is confused about how to apply a certain Scripture. But once the basics of dispensational theology are explained, they are no longer confused. Understanding and applying dispensations when you study your Bible clears up so much. (See bookmark inside front cover.)

The Bible is meant to be read literally, in context. Jesus took the Old Testament literally when He talked about creation, Adam and Eve, Noah's Ark, and Jonah being swallowed by the great fish. And all past prophecies were fulfilled literally, not figuratively. Therefore, we should also take the Bible literally, in context. Applying dispensations gives us that context.

For instance, the Bible says four times that the Millennial Reign of Christ on earth lasts 1000 years (Rev 20:4-7). That doesn't mean the 1000 years is symbolic for a "long period of time." It means what it says... it will last 1000 years. If you try to make it symbolic for a long period time, you're injecting man's sinfully tainted understanding into the interpretation.

God doesn't change, but He certainly does change how He deals with people

The Bible also says that in the millennium, the wolf and the lamb will lie in the grass together. Things will change and there will be no carnivorous instincts of animals (Isa. 11:6-7). This is another proof we're NOT in the millennium today! Yet the official doctrines of the Presbyterian, Lutheran, Church of Christ, and Catholic denominations (and many others) promote the heresy that we're living in the Millennium today.

God doesn't change, but He certainly does change how He deals with people through the different ages or time periods throughout history.

You can't argue that God didn't change through time how He dealt with people on the earth because He did (and will):

1) before and after the fall of man;
2) before and after the Flood;
3) before and after the Tower of Babel;
4) before and after the Cross;
5) before and after the Rapture;
6) before and after the Second Coming;
7) before and after the Great White Throne Judgment.

[See bookmark inside front cover.]

Therefore, it is a *fact* that God *does* change how He deals with people on the earth at different times through the ages. Dividing the Bible into Biblical Dispensations for context simply recognizes and applies this fact to Scriptural interpretation. And it clears up so many seemingly conflicting Scriptures.

Paul refers to the current Church Age dispensation as an "administration" that was hidden to the Jews but was now revealed:

> *"And to bring to light what is the administration of the mystery which **for ages has been hidden** in God who created all things;" Eph. 3:9*

Properly understanding and applying how God views these different time periods literally changed my life. Understanding dispensations allowed me to know when and where to apply every verse of Scripture. Without properly applying dispensations to understand the context of what the Lord is saying in Scripture, you're a ship without a rudder.

> *"As a result, we are no longer to be children, tossed here and there by waves and carried about by every wind of doctrine, by the trickery of men, by craftiness in deceitful scheming;" Eph. 4:14*

Later in this book, I write about the absurdity of not properly applying dispensations in your Bible study. It is titled "Satan's Lie: Do Everything Jesus Says." The point is that it is *impossible* for a Believer living in the Church Age to do everything Jesus said to do in the Gospels.

Properly understood, Matthew, Mark, Luke, and John are actually the end of the Old Testament, not the beginning of the New Testament. They are an account of Jesus' interaction with the Jews under the Law.

The Gospels are not specific instructions to those of us living in the Church Age. Instructions to those living in the Church Age are given by Paul in his 14 Epistles—his letters to the Christians in Rome, Romans; Corinth, 1st and 2nd Corinthians; Ephesus, Ephesians; etc.

I challenge anyone who holds a pre-wrath view of eschatology to find something Biblically wrong with that premise. And if you can't, you have no choice but to rethink your pre-wrath position. The title alone, purporting you should *not* do everything Jesus says to do, raises eyebrows because most people don't understand dispensations. They *assume* we're *supposed* to do what Jesus says to do in the Gospels.

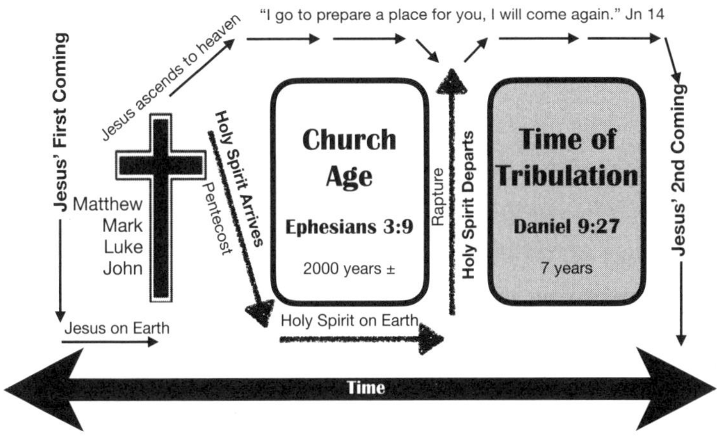

Millions have worn bracelets that proclaim "WWJD"—meaning that most of life's answers can be found by applying "What Would Jesus Do" to all of life's questions.

But with a proper contextual view of the Gospels, it's easy to see Jesus was not addressing those living in the Church Age, but rather, He was addressing Jews under the Law in a prior dispensation. He spoke to them differently because they did not have the discerning Spirit of God living in them. Matthew, Mark, Luke, and John are about events prior to the Cross.

The "Church Age," the dispensation in which we live, began only after Jesus' death and resurrection. It began when the Holy Spirit came to earth, and it will end when

He leaves at the Rapture. Therefore, the arrival and departure of the Holy Spirit on the earth are the bookends of the Church Age dispensation.

I think it's better to think of the Gospels as being the end of the Old Testament rather than the beginning of the New Testament. Only then can you fully appreciate the incredible Church Age characteristics. It's a special time on God's timeline unlike any other. As Peter said:

One key characteristic of dispensational theology is that the dispensational time periods can't overlap.

> *"...just as also our beloved brother Paul, according to the wisdom given him, wrote to you, as also in all his letters, speaking in them of these things, in which are some things hard to understand, which the untaught and unstable distort, as they do also the rest of the Scriptures, to their own destruction."*
> *2Pet. 3:15-16*

One key characteristic of dispensational theology is that the dispensational time periods can't overlap. A dispensation, by definition, must end before the next time dispensation can begin on God's calendar.

But the pre-wrath view has the Church Age crossing over into the Tribulation, into a new dispensation. That's absurd! You can't have two dispensations going on concurrently!!

But the biggest downside to the pre-wrath theory is that it robs Believers of the joy and expectation of the coming Rapture. The end of the Church Age is something to look forward to, not fear. We are to look for Jesus Christ, not the Antichrist!

> *"...let us run with endurance the race that is set before us,* ***fixing our eyes on Jesus,*** *the author and perfecter of faith..." Heb 12:1-2*

And lastly, here's one more problem with pre-wrath that is laughable. The pre-wrath position says that we, the Bride of Christ, will go through the first 3 1/2 years of Tribulation, meaning we'll be severely persecuted by God Himself before our wedding day with the Lord.

Really? Do you actually believe the Lord will unleash His wrath on the Church—the Bride of Christ—death and destruction, tearing us apart limb from limb, just before He marries us? Oh good grief! Not much to look forward to there! No, we, the "Bride of Christ," are to look forward to our marriage to the God of Love.

> *"Let us rejoice and be glad and give the glory to Him, for the marriage of the Lamb has come and His bride has made herself ready." Rev. 19:7*

CHAPTER TEN

WHAT PORNOGRAPHY DOES TO THE BRAIN

In His original creation, God designed guys to be responsive to visual stimulation. He then created women with curves to be visually enjoyed within the confines of marriage. And God blesses men when they find a mate.

> *"He who finds a wife finds a good thing and obtains favor from the LORD." Prov. 18:22*

Finding a Believer to love and cherish can be the best part of a Christian's life. And to top off the relationship, God blessed marriage with the act of sex. This was obviously part of His "fill-the-earth" strategy, but also sex is for pure physical enjoyment. God doesn't mince any words in this verse:

> *"Let your fountain be blessed, and rejoice in the wife of your youth. As a loving hind and a graceful doe, let her breasts satisfy you at all times; be exhilarated always with her love." Prov. 5:18-19*

Because Adam sinned and passed the sin nature down to every human, we live this life in a corrupted state that remains with us until we discard our earthly containers. And that sinful nature is so bad we can sin with a single glance from our eyes.

"The eye is the lamp of the body; so then if your eye is clear, your whole body will be full of light. But if your eye is bad, your whole body will be full of darkness. If then the light that is in you is darkness, how great is the darkness!" Matt. 6:22-23

...but I say to you that everyone who looks at a woman with lust for her has already committed adultery...

God warns us our eyes can be a major portal of sin. And if our sin remains unchecked, it leads progressively into great darkness.

Jesus even equated lusting with adultery:

"But I say to you that everyone who looks at a woman with lust for her has already committed adultery with her in his heart." Matt. 5:28

James said:

"But each one is tempted when he is carried away and enticed by his own lust." James 1:14

And John confirmed that all lusting comes from our age-old adversary, Satan.

> *"For all that is in the world, the lust of the flesh and the lust of the eyes and the boastful pride of life, is not from the Father, but is from the world." 1John 2:16*

Paul lists 15 "deeds of our flesh," i.e., sins we commit due to being deceived by Satan.

> *"Now the deeds of the flesh are evident, which are: immorality, impurity, sensuality, idolatry, sorcery, enmities, strife, jealousy, outbursts of anger, disputes, dissensions, factions, envying, drunkenness, carousing, and things like these," Gal. 5:19-21a*

Notice the very first thing on his warning list is immorality. The actual Greek word is *porneia,* where we get our English word pornography. The evolution of pornography took a giant leap when the Internet brought sex videos directly into our homes. *Playboy* and *Penthouse* magazines, termed soft-porn today, are no match for what's available on the Internet for free. And it is private, easy to access, and easy to hide.

The evolution of pornography took a giant leap when the Internet brought sex videos directly into our homes.

The fact is, Internet pornography is so accessible for free that as much as 40% of traditional porn suppliers, who were delivering porn via magazine or video, have gone out of business in the last ten years!

Josh McDowell said, "The greatest threat to the cause of Christ today is pervasive sexuality and pornography. We have lost control of the controls. With just one keystroke on a smartphone, iPad, or laptop, a child can open up some of the worst pornography and sexually graphic content you can imagine. There's never been such easy access in history."

Internet pornography is highly addictive. Consider these disturbing statistics:

- There are more than one billion pornographic webpages that are one click away for both adults and any child with a smart phone.

- On any given day, millions of people in the United States are sexually involved with the Internet. Over half of them claim to be Christians.

- The average age of first-time views of pornography is 10 years old.

- Eighty percent of 15-17 year olds have been exposed to hardcore porn.

- The adult pornography industry reports that 20-30 percent of their traffic comes from children (12 years old and younger).

- Over half of all Christian families report that pornography is a problem.
- Thirty percent of pastors admit to having viewed pornography in the last 30 days and 60 percent in the last six months. Most studies of pastors and Internet porn reveal between 60 and 70 percent are addicted!
- One out of every four online searches is for porn.

Over one-third of all churchgoing women have intentionally visited porn websites.

- In 56 percent of all divorce cases, one party had an obsessive interest in porn.
- Pornography use increases the risk of marital infidelity by more than 300 percent.
- When viewing pornography becomes an addiction:
  —40 percent of "sex addicts" lose their spouse.
  —58 percent suffer considerable financial loss.
  —About a third lose their jobs.
- And it's not all just men. Over one-third of all churchgoing women have intentionally visited porn websites.
- Over 50 percent of Christian men admit that pornography is a problem in their home. And that

doesn't count those who don't or won't admit it. But half is an incredible statistic. Some put the number as high as 70 percent.

Next time you're in church, look around you and think about the fact that probably well over half, maybe two thirds, of those sitting around you are dealing with pornography issues. Without restoration, they're in a no-win fight.

The Bible says....

> *"Can a man take fire in his bosom and his clothes not be burned? Or can a man walk on hot coals and his feet not be scorched?" Prov. 6:27-28*

And remember, Jesus said "looking" is no different than "doing."

> ***Can a man take fire in his bosom and his clothes not be burned?***

"...abstain from fleshly lusts which wage war against the soul." 1Pet. 2:11

The bottom line result is that when a person views porn, it diminishes normal sexual responses. Viewing porn requires scenes that are more sexually graphic to be sexually stimulating. Ultimately, in a marriage, viewing porn pushes the viewer to demand more and more kinky sex from his or her spouse for arousal.

Here at Compass we've noticed a marked increase of women calling about what to do about their husbands desiring anal sex. In desperation they're blurting out to us these problems before we can tell them that we don't do one-on-one counseling!!

Pornography and the Bible

Due to translations from Greek and Hebrew into English, the sin of pornography is unfortunately somewhat hard to notice in the Bible. Consider this verse:

> *"Marriage is to be held in honor among all, and the marriage bed is to be undefiled; for fornicators and adulterers God will judge." Heb. 13:4*

Marriage is to be held in honor among all, and the marriage bed is to be undefiled.

"Fornicators" is actually the Greek word *pornos.* So pornographic sin *is* quite explicit in Scripture, but the words used in translation are easily overlooked. The above verse could easily be translated "viewing pornography" instead of "fornicators."

Fifty Shades of Sin

We've even had a best-selling book (100 million+ copies sold), *Fifty Shades of Grey,* and the blockbuster movie by the same title. It's been described as an erotic romance novel, but this book and movie are simply pornography in your local theater.

Fifty Shades began as an e-book and, despite being universally declared "poorly written," the e-sales took off like a rocket and Vintage Books published it. The book doesn't have pictures, but the descriptions are so meticulous and descriptive that the images your mind assembles are no different than watching a porno movie.

> *"But immorality* [Greek - *"porneia"*/"pornography"] *or any impurity or greed must not even be named among you, as is proper among saints;" Eph. 5:3*

And the movie version, well, you're simply paying to watch porn in a theater. There's zero reason for a Believer to read the book, much less watch the movie.

> *"For this is the will of God, your sanctification; that is, that you abstain from sexual immorality* [Greek - *"pornos,"*/ "pornography"]*;" 1 Thes. 4:3*

Immorality or any impurity or greed must not even be named among you...

But *Fifty Shades* goes far deeper than simple pornography. It subtly sucks the reader into reading about abnormal sexual activities.The ungodly images will be seared on the readers' brains forever.

It also brings sado-masochism and bondage (referred to as "BDSM") into the minds of the readers as something that normal people could consider.

I'm not sure why, but *Fifty Shades* has a powerful appeal to women between 30 and 50, both single and married, drawing them into extremely graphic, pornographic word-pictures. Like playing with dynamite, it's a demonic portal into debauchery. So Believers should not even peek at the book's cover jacket. Run the other way!

> *"Flee immorality* [Greek - "porneia"]. *Every other sin that a man commits is outside the body, but the immoral* [Greek - "porneuo'] *man sins against his own body." 1 Cor 6:18*

Neurons that fire together, wire together.

Pornography and Your Brain

Viewing porn physically changes your brain! In the last two decades neuroplasticity has been discovered. "Neuro" means brain and "plasticity" means changeability. Scientists have discovered that our brain is constantly changing by laying down new pathways based on our experiences.

Neuroscientists have a saying, "Neurons that fire together, wire together." When brain cells (neurons) get activated by something you're watching, hearing or smelling, they release chemicals that strengthen the connections between those neurons.

An example of this is when you eat a delicious steak (or whatever your favorite food is). Your brain releases a chemical called dopamine that makes you feel good. Each time you eat a steak, a new pathway is created connecting steak with good feelings.

Or if you cuddle intimately with someone to whom you've become attracted, a different chemical is released (oxytocin) that increases bonding. The more time you spend with the person, the more pathways are developed.

Just like drug addiction, porn is no different than needing more and more drugs.

When a person looks at porn, even for a minute, the brain is flooded with the chemical dopamine. Pathways are developed. But with constant viewing, the brain fights back and begins restricting the overload. The result is that more and more porn is needed to get the good feeling.

And once you've started viewing porn regularly, if you stop for a while, your body will crave the good feeling that the chemical dopamine was bringing to you.

Yep, just like drug addiction, porn is no different than needing more and more drugs to get the same high. Or even more and more food to satisfy your hunger. In the exact same way, more and more porn is needed to get the same "porn high" from dopamine.

Just like a drug dealer will give away samples to "prime the pump/get you hooked," porn sites give away free samples to whet your appetite for more. And once the person is hooked, they will begin by viewing porn more often. Eventually, to satisfy his/her growing porn appetite, the person will move on and pay to see deeper and darker porn images.

There is no difference between being hooked on drugs and hooked on porn.

Believe it or not...it gets worse!

Once addiction grips the person, the part of the brain that helps you reason—helps you make good choices—is constantly being damaged.

The area affected is called the frontal lobe and the more that porn is viewed, the more damage it causes and the more difficult it becomes to make good choices and break free.

It becomes a vicious nonending cycle. View porn, make bad choices. View more porn, make more bad choices.

How To Stop Pornography Addiction

(What follows is our two cents on the subject, what we think someone should do if they are addicted to pornography. We are not counselors, just Bible researchers helping fellow Believers find answers in the Word of God. There are many other Christian counselors and Christian websites dealing with pornography addiction, and we recommend you prayerfully seek advice from more than one source.)

Thankfully, God promises that any Believer *can* break free of porn. Actually, the Believer can't, but Jesus can.

> *"I can do all things through Him who strengthens me." Phil 4:13*

Therefore, confess your sins to one another, and pray for one another...

By God's grace, the porn-damaged brain cells can be restored when someone gets away from sin. Repentance is the first step. Instead of looking to porn to meet your needs, you instead look to Jesus, Who is abundantly able! He knows your every sinful thought and desire. You can't, He can. To quit the cycle, you must begin with repentance, turning to Jesus to meet your needs.

> *"So I say to you, ask, and it will be given to you; seek, and you will find; knock, and it will be opened to you." Luke 11:9*

After repentance, the Scriptural remedy for restoration begins with prayer and accountability.

> *"And all things you ask in prayer, believing, you will receive." Matt. 21:22.*

> *"Therefore, confess your sins to one another, and pray for one another so that you may be healed." James 5:16*

If you're a Believer, you don't need to continually confess your sins to the Lord for forgiveness because He's already forgiven all of them through His blood on the Cross some 2000 years ago.

> *"Having canceled out the certificate of debt consisting of decrees against us, which was hostile to us; and He has taken it out of the way, having nailed it to the cross."*
> *Col. 2:14*

It's tremendously important to understand that *all* your sins—past, present and future—are behind you, nailed to the Cross 2000 years ago. When you pray to the Lord, He sees you as righteous. He has not quit loving you because of your addiction (sin). Getting off porn may save your marriage or your well-being. Notice the past-tense use of words in this verse:

> *"Such were some of you; but you were washed, but you were sanctified, but you were justified in the name of the Lord Jesus Christ and in the Spirit of our God."*
> *1Cor. 6:11*

...taking every thought captive to the obedience of Christ.

Biblical repentance starts with agreeing with the Lord that the Bible says you're in sin and that you know Jesus is the only permanent answer.

With an accountability partner to help keep you from relapsing, you set your sights on fully understanding Jesus' love for you. He desires for you to bring every thought into spiritual obedience.

"...taking every thought captive to the obedience of Christ."
2 Cor. 10:5b

Your goal is to get to the point that when you feel the desire for porn to meet your needs, you simply open your Bible, read of His grace, and trust Jesus to meet your needs. There is no better antidote than God's Word.

"Finally, brethren, whatever is true, whatever is honorable, whatever is right, whatever is pure, whatever is lovely, whatever is of good repute, if there is any excellence and if anything worthy of praise, dwell on these things."
Phil. 4:8

"And all things you ask in prayer, believing, you will receive." Matt. 21:22

When you begin to allow Him to rule your responses, you're on your way to enjoying the peace that surpasses all understanding!

"... walk by the Spirit, and you will not carry out the desire of the flesh." Gal. 5:16

If you don't have a pornography problem, people around you do, even if you don't know who they are. Odds are your pastor has a problem! So put your family and church leaders on your prayer list!

CHAPTER ELEVEN

EARTHQUAKES & VOLCANOES IN BIBLICAL PROPHECY

"...He is the living God and the everlasting King. At His wrath the earth quakes." Jer. 10:10

The wrath of God is a scary thing.

In 1 Chronicles 21, God's wrath was abundantly seen when King David disobeyed God and took a census of Israel. As punishment, God sent a pestilence that killed 70,000 Israeli men in three days!

In the future Tribulation we know that God will pour out His wrath on all those who take the Mark of the Beast, as well as on the entire earth.

"...If anyone worships the beast and his image, and receives a mark on his forehead or on his hand, he also will drink of the wine of the wrath of God..." Rev. 14:9,10

"Then I heard a loud voice from the temple, saying to the angels, 'Go and pour out on the earth the seven bowls of the wrath of God.'" Rev. 16:1

Believers living today in the Church Age, thankfully, have already been judged.

Prior to Noah, the earth was so wicked that God decided to, in essence, start over.

"For God has not destined us for wrath, but for obtaining salvation through our Lord Jesus Christ," 1Thes. 5:9

But until we exit this earth and receive our new containers, we must live on a fallen planet, Satan's temporary sinful domain. He's called:

"...the god of this world..." 2 Cor. 4:4

"...the ruler of this world..." John 12:31

And the problems coming from tornadoes, hurricanes, tsunamis, and volcanoes fall on both Believers and non-Believers alike.

But where did all these weather problems come from that we have today? If the earth was good when it was created, they would have had to come about *after* Adam sinned. It did, and our bad weather is rooted in sin.

Prior to Noah, the earth was so wicked that God decided to, in essence, start over. With the exception of Noah's family of eight, God destroyed the earth with a *global* Flood.

Prior to the Flood, the weather was perfect on a perfectly created planet.

> *"God saw all that He had made and behold, it was very good..." Gen. 1:31*

It had never rained. There were no thunderstorms, no floods, no hurricanes, no death, etc. Just an everyday mist watered the earth.

> *"Now no shrub of the field was yet in the earth, and no plant of the field had yet sprouted, for the LORD God had not sent rain upon the earth;... But a mist used to rise from the earth and water the whole surface of the ground." Gen. 2:5,6*

Later, when God flooded the earth to deal with sin, the physical ramifications changed the weather. Here's how:

When God flooded the earth, the Bible says water came from both above *and* below the surface of the earth.

> *"...all the fountains of the great deep burst open, and the floodgates of the sky were opened." Gen. 7:11*

Flood water also came from the sky, and some Christian scientists have theorized that prior to the Flood, a huge vapor canopy engulfed the earth. The theory continues that this canopy filtered the sun's rays and that's why many people lived so long prior to the Flood.

However, other scientists contend that a vapor canopy would have turned the planet into a greenhouse and therefore the water vapor theory, to them, has no credibility. But regardless of how much came from above the earth, most of the water that flooded the planet came from below.

It took a lot of water to flood this planet. Logically, "fountains" being plural, there were many places around the earth where water burst through the earth's surface in enormous amounts.

Recently scientists have discovered evidence of a vast water reservoir trapped hundreds of miles beneath the surface of the earth. There's apparently a lot more water under the earth's crust than above it!

It's possible that the portals through the earth's crust are the volcanoes we see today. Often there is even a lake at the top of the volcano, formed from water below.

> *"The water prevailed more and more upon the earth, so that all the high mountains everywhere under the heavens were covered." Gen. 7:19*

So the question is, how did the water cover the "high" mountains?

The answer is that there were no extremely high mountains at the time of the Flood. The high mountains we have today came after the initial flooding of the earth, as we will see later in this chapter.

The first thing to realize is that over 70 percent of the earth is covered with water.

In the satellite photo below, the visible earth is almost all water.

If the earth's surface was spread out perfectly flat, there's enough water in the oceans to cover the globe to a depth of about two miles!

When the earth was flooded from below, the tremendous amount of sediment released began to settle on the bottom. The heaviest particles settled first, then the next heaviest, continuing until the lightest dirt particles and sediment settled on top.

The result is that today, all over the earth where there is a visible cutaway of a mountain, you can easily see these layers. This is clearly seen in the picture below where the light chalky sediment is the top layer and the heaviest particles are at the bottom.

Evolutionists say these layers were laid down over millions of years. Of course, they can't explain why the heaviest layers are at the bottom and the lightest layers are at the top. Nor can they explain how the same fossils are in all layers!

But there are two weight-graduated layerings found all over the planet. This is because after the earth was flooded and the first horizontal layers were formed, God then moved the ground vertically to make the mountains and valleys.

> "*You covered* [the earth] *with the deep as with a garment; The waters were standing above the mountains. At Your rebuke they fled. At the sound of Your thunder they hurried away.* <u>*The mountains rose; the valleys sank*</u> *down to the place which You established for them. You set a boundary that they may not pass over, so that they will not return to cover the earth." Ps. 104:6-9*

Secular Layering Display at the Grand Canyon

"Whatever the LORD pleases, He does, in heaven and in earth, in the seas and in all deeps." Psa. 135:6

So the newly laid down horizontal layers were pushed up, churning up the dirt in the water a second time.

As would be expected, this second layering has the heaviest particles forming the bottom layers and the lightest layers forming the top layers—perfectly matching the Genesis Flood story.

In this close-up picture of the display, we see the gray stone at the bottom is the original creation bedrock. (See #1)

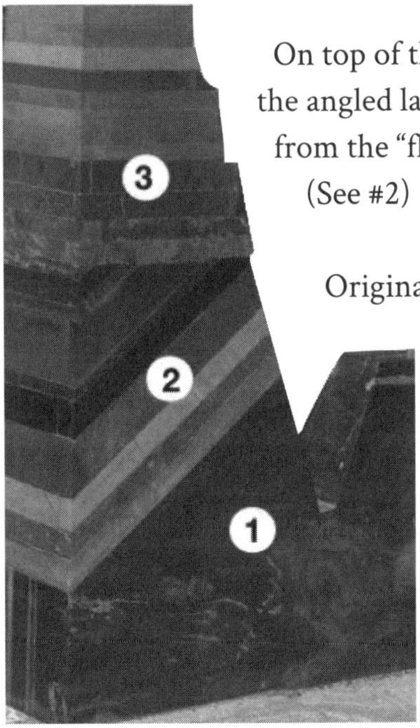

On top of the original "creation rock," the angled layers are the layers formed from the "flooding from below." (See #2)

Originally these layers were laid down horizontally but were pushed up at an angle when God raised the mountains and lowered the valleys.

As the mountains were raised, it caused more turbulence in the water, which, in turn, caused additional settling of layers ... hence the top horizontal layers on the display. (See #3)

A Recap

In the beginning, God created the earth, the original earth (1). Then God flooded the earth from below. Lots of dirt, rocks, and sediment came up with the water from below. The layers on top of original earth (2) were laid down horizontally from all that turbulence and debris as the water poured through the volcano portals to flood the earth.

Layers of sediment laid down from the flooding of the Earth

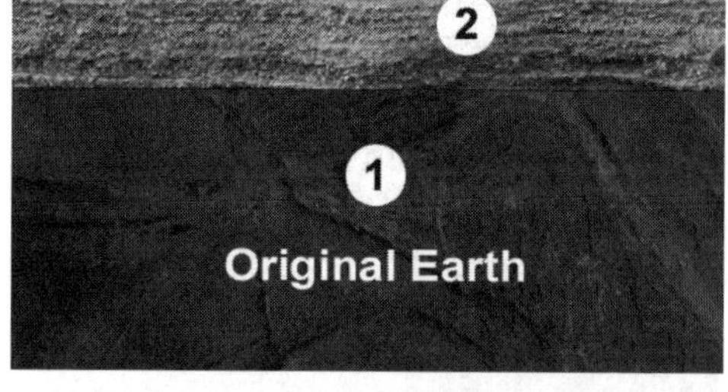

This is confirmed by the fact that the layers at the bottom have the heaviest particles and the layers at the top the lightest.

But then God raised mountains and lowered the valleys, pushing up the sedimentary layers (2). This again caused a tremendous amount of dirty water and sediment to be stirred up. And this sediment again settled to the bottom, forming new horizontal layers (3).

Isn't it amazing that the secular geological display you see at the Grand Canyon confirms the Biblical account of the worldwide Flood about 4500 years ago!

The Bible says the earth will never again be flooded, a promise sealed with the rainbow in the sky. This is referred to as the Noahic Covenant.

> *"...never again shall the water become a flood to destroy all flesh. When the bow is in the cloud, then I will look upon it, to remember the everlasting covenant between God and every living creature of all flesh that is on the earth." Gen 9:15,16*

But earthquakes are a different story. The biggest earthquake yet is still in the future.

> *"And there were flashes of lightning and sounds and peals of thunder; and there was a great earthquake, such as there had not been since man came to be upon the earth, so great an earthquake was it, and so mighty." Rev. 16:18*

> *"And every island fled away, and the mountains were not found." Rev. 16:20*

Wow! In the future there is *one* earthquake bigger than any earthquake that has ever happened on earth. God will flatten the steep mountains. No wonder men will be weak-kneed as they see the wrath of God on full display.

But all things work together ultimately for Believers. The high and steep mountains from Noah's Flood cause irregular wind pattens on the earth.

As the earth turns, the irregular and high mountains cause abnormal wind currents, which account for our weather problems today.

But when all the steep mountains are reduced to rolling hills from that *huge* earthquake, the world's weather will change also—back to what it was like before the Flood.

Therefore, when Jesus returns to reign on the earth as King of Kings, there will be no worries of tornadoes, tsunamis and hurricanes.

(And if you want to see an incredible view of the original creation rock with both groups of layers on top, join us on one of our annual Grand Canyon trips.)

The Big Volcano

There have been several earthquakes in Yellowstone National Park through the years, and they're increasing in frequency in the last few decades.

It turns out that there is, today, one *gigantic* volcano under Yellowstone National Park. It's not noticeable too much from the ground because of its size. The walls are 30 to 50 miles apart and appear only as distant mountains.

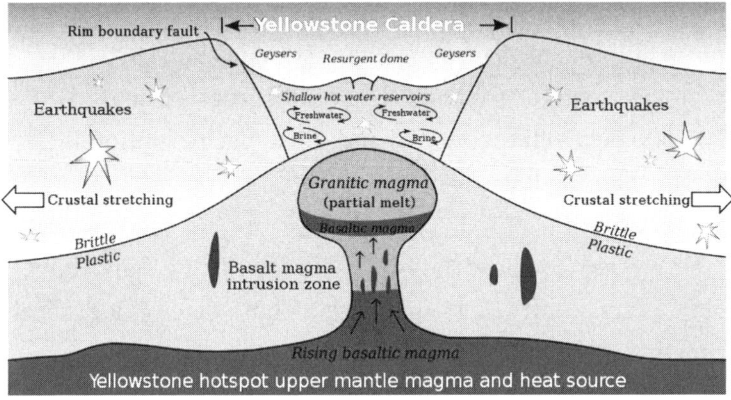

This volcano has had three massive explosions in the past, and geologists have found the remains of the debris fields of each eruption.

Notice the size of the debris field from the Mt. St. Helen's explosion in 1980 in Washington State and Idaho. We thought that was a big volcanic explosion! But the largest Yellowstone explosion carried ash and debris 1500 miles, to Canada, Mexico, and all the way to Mississippi!

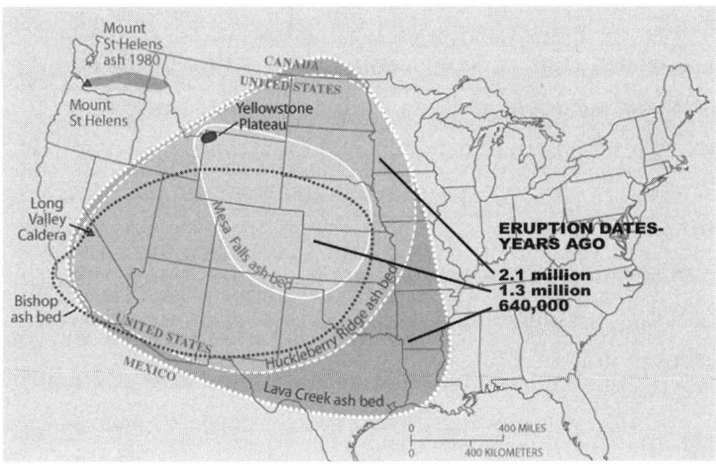

Also note that geologists estimate the eruptions took place millions of years ago. They estimate about 800,000 years between the first and the second eruption, and 700,000 between the second and third. Each eruption is larger than the last.

However, we know the Bible says the earth is only about 6000 years old. If you roughly apply those dates to a Biblical timeline, it would look like this:

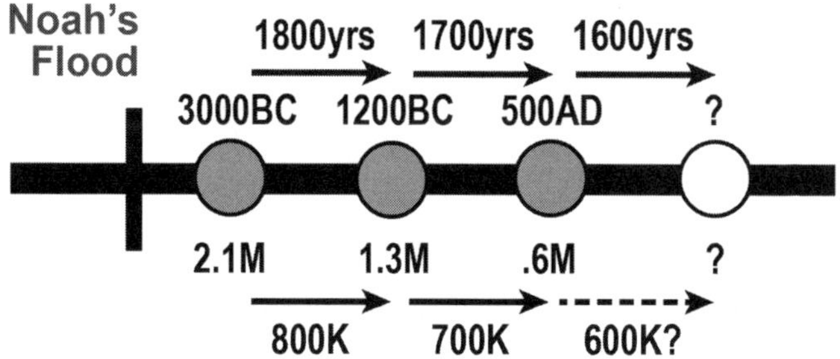

This last graphic is obviously not scientific. And I'm not trying to be doom and gloom. But it *is* interesting that we're probably in that window of the expected fourth Yellowstone volcanic explosion, and maybe even past due!

And since we know that huge earthquakes *are* part of the tribulation judgments, it is logical this *could* be part of the coming judgments.

"And there will be great earthquakes, and in various places plagues and famines; and there will be terrors and great signs from heaven." Luke 21:11

And if the Tribulation is near, so is the Rapture!

CHAPTER TWELVE

WHEN JESUS WENT TO HELL

Today Believers immediately go to heaven when they die because of what Jesus did on the Cross (2Cor. 5:8). His sacrificial, shed blood makes it possible. But it wasn't always like that.

Prior to Jesus dying on the Cross, Old Testament Believers could *not* go to heaven when they died. This was because their sins were not yet paid for by the Messiah. They had to wait; they had to first be cleansed and made perfect.

When Old Testament Believers died, they went to a place in the center of the earth. It had two parts: Paradise and Hades. Here the Old Testament Believers waited on the Messiah to redeem them with His blood.

Once the Messiah died on the Cross, Believers then *could* go to heaven when they died because they were no longer forbidden to enter heaven as they were cleansed by the blood of the Lamb.

We derive this information from the verses about the Rich Man and Lazarus in Luke 16:19-31. This glimpse into what is called the Bottomless Pit in Revelation 9:1-2 is not a parable but rather an actual event. And a bit eerie at that!

[If you're not familiar with the Luke 16 story, take a moment to give it a quick read.]

Before the Cross, those who died and were saved by faith by trusting in a future Messiah went to Paradise. Scripture says they were in "comfort." That's good because some of them had to be there for thousands of years waiting on the Messiah!

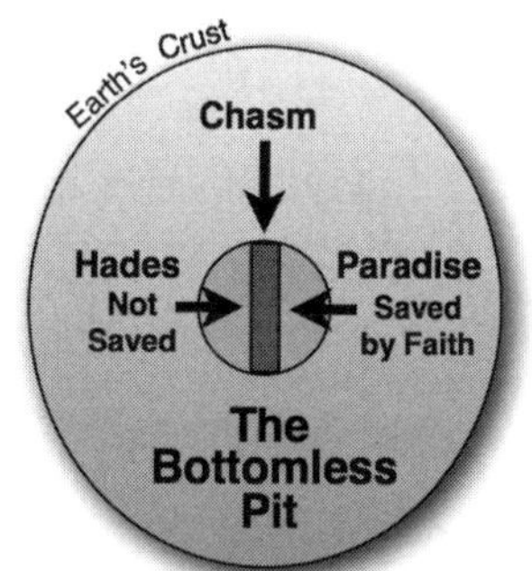

Those who were not saved by faith went to the other side of the Bottomless Pit—Hades—where they were in "agony," "torment," and "flame." Not good! At the end of the age they will all be judged and cast into hell with the devil and his angels. Hell will make Hades look like a weenie roast.

After the Cross

Today when Believers die they go straight to heaven as their sins have been permanently paid for by Jesus' shed blood some 2000 years ago—totally escaping the torturous flames of both Hades and Hell.

"I ... prefer rather to be absent from the body and to be at home with the Lord." 2Cor. 5:8

But there was another incredible time period—just after Jesus died on the Cross and before He ascended to heaven. He had to redeem those in Paradise waiting to go to heaven!

Therefore He "descended" to the good side of the Bottomless Pit, into Paradise, and took all those Old Testament Believers with Him to heaven.

"(Now this expression, 'He ascended,' what does it mean except that He also had descended into the lower parts of the earth?)" Eph. 4:9

Wow, think about it, all the Old Testament saints from Adam and Eve to Isaiah to Daniel... all of them were in one huge room where every direction was up. Some had been waiting there for almost 4000 years!

And then Jesus finally arrives! That earth-shattering shout of exultation by so many excited Believers may have been the earthquake that caused the curtain to split in the Jewish Temple!

Jesus had come to redeem that which was His. And as if God wanted to prove He has a sense of humor, some of those traveling from Paradise in the center of the earth to heaven above the earth stopped off on the earth's surface!

> *"The tombs were opened, and many bodies of the saints who had fallen asleep* [died] *were raised; and coming out of the tombs after His resurrection they entered the holy city and appeared to many." Matt. 27:52-53*

Amazingly, some of the Old Testament saints stopped on earth as they passed through the crust. Can you imagine that? Some could have been dead only a few days. Some could have died 3000 years earlier. Yet there they were, walking around the earth, talking to people. Imagine *that* conversation!

Jew #1: "Hey, Zechariah, I thought you died!"

Amazingly, some of the Old Testament saints stopped on earth as they passed through the crust. Can you imagine that?

Jew #2: "Yeah, I did die but had to wait for the shed blood of Jesus to cover my sins before I could go to heaven. And you won't believe who's going to heaven... and who isn't!"

Ok, I speculated a little bit with that last line. But it just boggles my mind that some Jews living at the time of Christ saw people who had died hundreds or thousands of years before and had been waiting on the Messiah in Paradise!

And, as if this study couldn't get any stranger, the Bottomless Pit will also play a role in the future Tribulation period. Apparently all the demons locked up from the Flood, the really, really bad ones, will be released back into the earth during the Tribulation as part of God's wrath. (Rev 9:2)

Two thoughts on those demons....

First, Hades would not be a good place to be, even though it was not yet the eternal Hell in which they will eventually reside. In addition to dealing with the horrific hot flames without water, those poor people will also have to deal with those grotesque demons torturing them night and day.

Second, if you miss the Rapture, your worst nightmare begins. You might as well be in Hell. It will be so painful that you'll think it would be better to be crushed by rocks and die!

> *"And they said to the mountains and to the rocks, 'Fall on us and hide us from the presence of Him who sits on the throne, and from the wrath of the Lamb'"; Rev. 6:16*

> *"And in those days men will seek death and will not find it; they will long to die, and death flees from them." Rev. 9:6*

For those who willingly oppose God and reject His mercy, there is no hope. But His love is *so* great that Scripture tells us that He is not willing that any should perish. Yay!

"The Lord is not slow about His promise, as some count slowness, but is patient toward you, not wishing for any to perish but for all to come to repentance." 2 Pet 3:9

And, gratefully, He has no pleasure in the death of lost sinners.

"For I have no pleasure in the death of anyone who dies," declares the Lord GOD." Ezek 18:32

What a great privilege and comfort to be able to turn to Him now and know that we can look forward with excitement and not terror. Our future is better than anything we can imagine!

"...things which eye has not seen and ear has not heard, and ***which have not entered the heart of man,*** *all that God has prepared for those who love Him." 1 Cor. 2:9*

That's exciting! Heaven will be better than anything we can conceive in our brain. I can think of a lot of A-Plus situations that heaven might be like, but it's better than anything I can imagine!

What a privilege to live on this earth knowing that truth!

CHAPTER THIRTEEN

RUSSIA'S FUTURE HUMILIATING DEFEAT

God will openly humble Russia in the future. Pride comes before the fall. Is the prophesied defeat dead ahead? Yes!

Why God Gave Us Bible Prophecy

With over 25% of the Bible written in prophetic prose, there's apparently a good reason God gave us so much Bible prophecy to study. Yet for some strange reason many churches today have simply quit teaching anything to do with prophecy.

The main reason God gave us Bible prophecy is to prove that the rest of the Bible is 100% accurate. This separates the Bible from the Koran, the Book of Mormon, and every other book in the universe because only God can predict the future.

And since 100% of all past prophecies were fulfilled literally, we know the future prophecies will also be fulfilled literally. If God says the Millennium is 1000 years long, it doesn't mean "a long time." It means just what it says, in context.

Prophecy is Comforting

Another reason God gave us Bible prophecy is to be a comfort to Believers. After penning several sentences discussing the Rapture, Paul gives us this command:

> ***We're comforted by knowing God is in control and that nothing is happening He didn't already know.***

"Therefore comfort one another with these words." 1Thes. 4:18

We're comforted by knowing God is in control and that nothing is happening He didn't already know about and allow. God can't learn and therefore He is never surprised.

There is not one thing happening in this country, or in your personal life, of which He wasn't fully aware and expecting.

But God is not mocked, and in the future His wrath is coming again on this earth.

"Then I heard a loud voice from the temple, saying to the seven angels, 'Go and pour out on the earth the seven bowls of the wrath of God.'" Rev. 16:1

But we're comforted because Bible prophecy tells us we're not going to have to endure God's wrath in the future seven-year Tribulation because, thankfully, Believers are raptured away first.

> *"For God has* <u>*not*</u> *destined us for wrath, but for obtaining salvation through our Lord Jesus Christ," 1Thes. 5:9*

But it's interesting that just after Paul discusses Rapture in his letter to the Thessalonians, God inspired him to write:

> *"For you yourselves know full well that the day of the Lord will come just like a thief in the night. While they are saying, 'Peace and safety!' then destruction will come upon them suddenly like labor pains upon a woman with child, and they will not escape. But you, brethren, are not in darkness, that the day would overtake you like a thief;" 1Thes. 5:2-4*

This statement runs parallel with Jesus' words that just before the Rapture it will be *just like* the Days of Noah (Matt. 24:37-39).

We're comforted because Bible prophecy tells us we're not going to have to endure God's wrath.

In the Days of Noah the pagan world had no idea the worldwide Flood was about to happen, despite Noah's life-long preaching (2 Pet. 2:5).

Noah Knew

It's easy to see that Noah could quite easily tell when the Flood was getting close. When he and his sons had finished loading all the food and water and the animals began showing up in twos and sevens, Noah obviously could see that time was short. That day didn't overtake him like a thief in the night. Noah saw the signs.

So it's not wrong to look at the Biblical signs regarding the latter days. It *is* wrong to set a specific date in the future.

> ***When God closes the Church Age dispensation (time period), He will again make Israel His primary focus.***

Israel Is God's Prophetic Timepiece

Therefore as we properly assess the prophetic signs regarding Jesus' return, the very first thing we should do is look at Israel. Israel is God's prophetic timepiece.

When God closes the Church Age dispensation (time period), He will again make Israel His primary focus as He shakes the earth to its core. So what are the main latter-day Biblical signs tied into Israel? Here's a big one...

The Northern Invasion Led By Russia

In Ezekiel 37, written over 2500 years ago, God promised to miraculously bring the dispersed Jews back to their land from the four corners of the earth after having been dispersed for almost two millennia.

"Then it will happen on that day that the Lord will again recover the second time with His hand the remnant of His people, who will remain... And He will lift up a standard for the nations, and assemble the banished ones of Israel, and will gather the dispersed of Judah from the four corners of the earth." Is. 11:11-12

The first Jewish return was from their Babylonian exile, 586-538 BC. Their second return is from being scattered around the world in 70 AD, after rejecting their Messiah in 33 AD.

The Jews started returning from this worldwide banishment in 1917 and became a nation again in 1948.

"God has not rejected His people whom He foreknew." Rom. 11:2a

In Ezekiel 38 and 39 Ezekiel prophesied that after Israel was back in her land, she would be invaded from the north by a group of nations led by Gog/Magog, and most Bible scholars identify this to be Russia. Listed in the group of the accompanying countries is Persia, which in 1935 changed its name to Iran.

Russia Today In Syria

I believe the timing of this invasion is most likely to be post-Rapture. So when Russia instituted a new military draft for 150,000 conscripts and started operating militarily in Syria while working hand-in-hand with Iran, it doesn't take a rocket scientist to see that this is Bible prophecy being fulfilled literally.

The Missing Ingredient

But there still is one more prophecy to be fulfilled. The Bible says **the purpose of the Ezekiel 38/39 invasion is to capture Israel's riches.** Riches? What riches does Israel have that a sovereign nation would invade to capture? The Bible says Israel will have great riches in the last days. This is mentioned four times in two verses.

> *"To capture spoil and to seize plunder," Ezek. 38:12a*

> *"...Have you come to capture spoil? Have you assembled your company to seize plunder, to carry away silver and gold, to take away cattle and goods, to capture great spoil?" Ezek. 38:13*

Until recently, Israel had no natural resources like gold, silver, oil, or gas. This prompted Golda Meir, Israel's Prime Minister from 1969 to 1974, to famously say, "Moses dragged us through the desert for 40 years to bring us to the one place in the Middle East where there was no oil."

But that is changing and changing fast! And it's another reason to believe we're getting close to the Rapture. Israel has struck oil! After discovering an abundance of gas around the coasts of Israel, an oil exploration company has finally struck oil. After drilling over 500 dry wells, Afek Oil and Gas, a subsidiary of Genie Energy, confirmed it struck a significant oil reservoir in Israel in 2015.

The discovery is a monstrous layer of oil over 1000 feet thick. It is expected to be large enough to produce billions of gallons of oil for Israel, and it's believed that there's enough oil to both supply Israel's energy needs as a country and also begin exporting oil to Europe. Think that is sitting well with OPEC?

There'll come a time when Russia invades with Iran to get Israel's oil and whatever else she discovers...

Israel is playing down the oil discovery in the media so as not to give other Arab nations more incentive to come against her. But there'll come a time when Russia invades with Iran to get Israel's oil and whatever else she discovers in the land.

Russia Loses Badly

The Bible says this northern invasion fails miserably as it is God Himself who defeats the attacking nations:

> *"With pestilence and with blood I will enter into judgment with him; and I will rain on him and on his troops, and on the many peoples who are with him, a torrential rain, with hailstones, fire and brimstone." Ezek. 38:22*

> *"I will strike your bow from your left hand and dash down your arrows from your right hand. You will fall on the mountains of Israel, you and all your troops and the peoples who are with you; I will give you as food to every kind of predatory bird and beast of the field." Ezek. 39:3-4*

God Himself defeats Russia, not Israel. Four times in the above He says, "I will." Just like God wiped out entire armies of Israel's enemies in the Old Testament, God will *personally* defeat and humiliate Russia. And this prideful atheistic nation will know it was almighty God who defeated them!

> *"I will magnify Myself, sanctify Myself, and make Myself known in the sight of many nations; and they will know that I am the LORD." Ezek. 38:23*

This is a good reason that this battle will take place in the next dispensation, post-Rapture, because God's not personally wiping out nations with vengeance from the sky today. But the Rapture will change everything.

Notice that it's God Himself who defeats Russia. Not Israel.

The Great Sword

This invasion will include nuclear weapons.

> *"And another, a red horse, went out; and to him who sat on it, it was granted to take peace from the earth, and that men would slay one another; and a great sword was given to him." Rev. 6:4*

> *"...their flesh will rot while they stand on their feet, and their eyes will rot in their sockets, and their tongue will rot in their mouth." Zech. 14:12b*

Between the "great sword" and their "flesh rotting" before they fall to the ground, it reeks of a nuclear attack! So Iran *will* have nuclear weapons, and Russia, of course, already has them, and they'll try to use them against Israel.

God's Purpose For Crushing Russia

Post-Rapture, the earth will be in a new dispensation. This new time period will be much different than the Church Age. The Restraining Power of the Holy Spirit will be gone (2Thes. 2:6-7).

People will be saved by faith during the Tribulation, just like before the Church Age, but those living in this new time will see destructive things worldwide that we never dreamed of seeing today.

People will be saved by faith during the Tribulation, just like before the Church Age.

And most interesting is that the purpose of this crushing defeat of Israel's invading enemies is to show both the people of Israel and the people of the world that God is not dead, but rather He is in complete control and is again actively defending Israel!

> *"My holy name I will make known in the midst of My people Israel; and I will not let My holy name be profaned anymore. And the nations will know that I am the LORD, the Holy One in Israel." Ezek. 39:7*

With the United States having been decimated by the Rapture, this incredible victory by Israel over Russia and her cohorts will give Israel the confidence to fulfill this prophecy about militarily taking out *all* of her closest-in-proximity enemies.

> *"In that day I will make the clans of Judah like a fire-pot among pieces of wood and a flaming torch among sheaves, so they will consume on the right hand and on the left all the surrounding peoples, while the inhabitants of Jerusalem again dwell on their own sites in Jerusalem." Zech. 12:6*

All of this wholesale destruction of the Arabs by Israel will bring the Middle East to its knees. Those nations next on Israel's hit list will beg for the world to stop Israel's carnage.

All of this wholesale destruction of the Arabs by Israel will bring the Middle East to its knees.

The Seven-Year Peace Plan

The remaining Arab nations, and the rest of the world, promise the sky if Israel will just stop the destruction. Israel will reluctantly agree to a seven-year peace agreement between Israel, five Western European nations, and five Eastern European nations (Dan. 2, 9:27).

The author of this peace agreement will be an unheralded man who comes out of nowhere. But the world is so impressed with his deft negotiation skills that tamed a previously untamable situation, they blindly support anything and all he does. More and more power is handed over to him (Dan. 10:23).

Thus begins the Great Tribulation, which is also called the Time of Jacob's Trouble and/or the 70th Week of Daniel, which ushers in God's undiluted wrath on earth. (See bookmarks inside front cover.)

Now is an exciting time to be alive and watch the 2500-year-old prophecies unfold before our very eyes.

As the latter-days Bible prophecies play out, it will be more and more obvious that a dispensational change might be just ahead!

Pray for eternal witnessing opportunities!

CHAPTER FOURTEEN

HOME OF THE BRAVE?

To most of us, it's hard to believe that someone would sit or kneel, not stand, for the national anthem. God blessed this nation more than any other and to protest perceived unjust treatment is stupid... especially since the blood of past veterans fighting for our flag is what gives them the right to protest! Apparently they don't know much about how we got the National Anthem. This is the story.

In the War of 1812, America was again fighting her mother country, Great Britain. Britain had lost the American War of Independence in 1783, but now 29 years later, she was determined to take America back as a British possession.

In Europe, Napoleon had been defeated and all the seasoned British troops were sent en masse to the United States in order to take back the land and its rich tax base.

The initial battles were fought in the north, in and around the Canadian border. But in August 1814, the

British invaded Washington, D.C., burning and looting the White House, the Capitol, the Treasury, War Department, and Navy Yard. President James Madison and the entire U.S. government had to flee the city and eventually ended up hiding in Brookeville, Maryland.

It was a dark and pivotal moment for the new Republic with our capital in Washington destroyed.

American troops were demoralized and were easily defeated in successive battles around the Washington area. The British spent several days looting tons of merchandise from city merchants. In the countryside, farms were looted for food and other provisions. Those who resisted were arrested and taken as prisoners of war.

It was a dark and pivotal moment for the new Republic. With our capital in Washington destroyed, our government leaders on the run and our troops in disarray, the British turned their sights to Baltimore for a knock-out blow. The British believed victory was at hand.

On Sept. 12, 1814, 5,000 British troops headed by land from Washington to Baltimore, only 35 miles away. They met 3,000 American troops about five miles outside Baltimore.

The Americans initially engaged the British in battle, but then retreated as a stalling tactic to allow time for more American troops to arrive.

At the same time, a large flotilla from the British Royal Navy was sailing through the Chesapeake Bay to attack Baltimore from the sea. It included five (of eight) massive siege artillery ships Britain had in its navy and used to pulverize cities from the sea. So the only thing between the British Navy vessels and Baltimore was Fort McHenry. If Fort McHenry was destroyed, Baltimore would be a sitting duck and the British would win the war.

During this time, a young lawyer was commissioned to make contact with the British about a prisoner exchange. One of the prisoners of war, Dr. William Beanes, was a prominent physician. He was arrested at his farm outside Washington, D.C., for resisting the British.

The lawyer was able to negotiate the release for all the prisoners except Beanes. Eventually it was established that Beanes was a civilian non-combatant and could be released once the British had conquered Baltimore. So the lawyer and Beanes were sequestered on a ship about eight miles from Fort McHenry.

A young lawyer was commissioned to make contact with the British about a prisoner exchange.

From the ship, using a telescope, the lawyer could see the massive fleet sailing up Chesapeake Bay toward the tiny fort with the United States flag boldly flying over the fort's ramparts. But the prospects of repelling such an onslaught were grim, to say the least. It appeared the fledgling nation was about to be conquered less than 40 years after its breakaway from England.

The British fleet arrived, and as twilight began to fall, there was a haze over the water, typical of sunsets in Baltimore. The British Admiral in charge of the fleet, Admiral Cochrane, maneuvered his ships into position and began to relentlessly shell the small fort with the large American flag, unleashing his cannons on the helpless occupants.

Every time a bomb would explode near the flag, the lawyer could see the flag was still there.

The lawyer recounted later that the explosive sounds from the British cannons were so deafening that you couldn't even hear to talk. There was almost no pause from the massive cannon fire as the ships moved one after another into position to fire everything they had at the fort. The sky was pitch black but was lit up by the yellow and red bursting bombs.

Every time a bomb would explode near the flag, the lawyer could see the flag was still there. He knew the thing that sets Americans apart from all other people in the world is that they would rather die standing up than live on their knees.

Brave Americans died that night, refusing to surrender. When sunrise came, there was a heavy mist over the water and the fort in the distance, and as the morning light enveloped the area, even though the flag pole itself was leaning heavily to the side, the lawyer could see the shredded American flag still flying proudly.

In the end, the British concluded the fort could not be breached and, therefore, moving ships past it to attack Baltimore was impossible. Our American ground troops, inspired by those giving up their lives from the onslaught of the British cannons at Fort McHenry, won a decisive victory and Baltimore was saved.

The British were also dealing with the fact that the American citizens were heavily armed and therefore unmanageable. Since the British troops wore bright red uniforms and tended to walk in a straight line, they made easy targets for a well-armed nation who had enough sense to shoot from behind trees and rocks.

This was the turning point in the War of 1812. America has never since been at risk of being conquered by an invasive enemy army.

The lawyer was so moved by those brave men that he wrote a poem titled "Defence of Fort McHenry."

The first verse of his poem reads:

"O say can you see, by the dawn's early light.
What so proudly we hail'd at the twilight's last gleaming.
Whose broad stripes and bright stars, through the perilous fight.

O'er the ramparts we watched, were so gallantly streaming.
And the rockets' red glare, the bombs bursting in air,
gave proof through the night, that our flag was still there.
O say does that star-spangled banner yet wave,
O'er the land of the free and the home of the brave?"

The lawyer in this story was, of course, Francis Scott Key. And his poem eventually became the words for our national anthem. And do notice that the last line in the first verse ends with a question mark ("?")!

And what revisionist history writers don't want you to know is the last verse to that original poem because it mentions God's protection of America, His power that divinely preserved this nation and that God is Who we trust, not ourselves. Fascinatingly it reads:

"Oh! thus be it ever, when freemen shall stand
Between their loved home and the war's desolation!
Blest with victory and peace, may the heav'n rescued land
Praise the Power that hath made and preserved us a nation.
Then conquer we must, when our cause it is just,
And this be our motto: "In God is our trust."
And the star-spangled banner in triumph shall wave
O'er the land of the free and the home of the brave!"

And do notice that the last verse ends with an exclamation mark ("!") instead of a question mark ("?") like the first verse. The last line of the last verse answered the previous question.

As it's often been said, freedom is not free. Throughout the history of this country, we have paid the price for freedom with the blood of our countrymen. Roughly two million men and women have died in all wars since 1776.

So, praise the Lord that we've had the incredible blessings afforded only by the blood of those who fought and died for this country.

So don't take lightly praying for this nation. Satan hates the United States.

It is also interesting to note that the number of those in the U.S. who supported the United States over those who supported Great Britain in the War for Independence (1776-1784) were much less than 50 percent. Estimates range from a low of 15 to a high of 40 percent!

It's no wonder the new Constitution made provisions to protect minorities! We were founded as a Republic, not a Democracy!

So don't take lightly praying for this nation. Satan hates the United States. He hates Christians, Bible teaching churches, Biblical prayers, evangelism, mission work, Christian marriages ... basically anything good. He is total evil and he's doing all he can to mitigate true Believer's influence.

And never forget that we're not up against people. It's not the Muslims we're fighting against. It's not liberals. It's not flesh, period. They're all just duped by the master duper who's had 6000 years of practice.

> *"Put on the full armor of God, so that you will be able to stand firm against the schemes of the devil. For our struggle is not against flesh and blood, but against the rulers, against the powers, against the world forces of this darkness, against the spiritual forces of wickedness in the heavenly places. Therefore, take up the full armor of God, so that you will be able to resist in the evil day, and having done everything, to stand firm." Eph. 6:11-13*

And you can see Satan's hatred more and more as Americans and Christians are being openly murdered worldwide. And if the Lord tarries long enough, we will probably see Believers' rights erode here in the United States.

But regardless of what the Lord allows to happen in this country, never forget that we've already won the battle through Jesus' blood. Our most important assets are God's Word and our personal witness.

As we've said often, the only thing that truly matters in this life is who goes to heaven and who goes to hell. So our prayers should be, "Use us, Lord!"

CHAPTER FIFTEEN

WHO ARE THE 144,000 IN REVELATION?

One of the most overlooked characteristics of the future seven-year Tribulation period is that the Gospel of Jesus Christ will be preached to the entire world. People are given the stark choice to follow Jesus or Satan. All through the book of Revelation we see the Gospel being preached to the whole world. (See inset, below.)

The Bible describes the Tribulation as an intense evangelistic period in and among the catastrophic judgments by God. And the astonishing purveyors of the Gospel will be none other than Jews! 144,000 Jews will be given instant Holy Spirit illumination—12,000 from each of the 12 Jewish tribes (Rev. 7:4). They are singers (Rev 14:3). But more interestingly

> *"...an eternal gospel..." Revelation 14:6*
> *"...the testimony of Jesus..." Revelation 12:17*
> *"...their faith in Jesus." Revelation 14:12*
> *"...the witness of Jesus." Revelation 17:6*
> *"...against the Lamb," Revelation 17:14*
> *"...blood of the Lamb..." Revelation 12:11*
> *"...the song of the Lamb..." Revelation 15:3*
> *"...testimony of Jesus..." Revelation 19:10*
> *"...in the blood of the Lamb." Revelation 7:14*
> *"...the Lamb..." Revelation 7:17*
> *"...follow the Lamb..." Revelation 14:4*

these Jewish men are also unmarried virgins! (Rev. 14:4) So if we are living in the last days, let's say between two seconds and 20 years prior to Rapture, who are these 144,000 Jewish male virgins, and where do they come from?

Today in Israel about 80 percent of the population consider themselves as "secular" Jews. In talking to scores of secular Jewish people on our trips to Israel, I found that they usually observe Passover and the Day of Atonement. But for the most part, they don't go to synagogue on Shabbat (Saturday) and don't know what to think about the miracles of the Old Testament. And prior to marriage, dating is similar to nonbelievers in the U.S.A., with most having sex prior to marriage.

There are some who consider themselves as "Orthodox" Jews. They will wear the *yamika* (sometimes referred to as "kippah," [the cap]) to keep something between them and God. They believe the Bible is the Word of God, go to synagogue on Shabbat, and, of course, celebrate the seven Jewish feasts. But they dress normally, have no problem with using birth control, serve in the army, and work for a living. They also support the State of Israel.

And there is a third group, a most curious oddity, referred to as the "Ultra-Orthodox" Jews, or *Haredi* in Hebrew (means "one who trembles in awe of God"). Oh my gosh, they are a sight to see. Numbering about 1.3 million (800,000 in Israel), the men all dress in black suits with white shirts and a hat. The type of hat worn depends on the particular order to which they belong. The largest group of them live in Jerusalem.

They vote as a bloc, sort of like a third party, and it's almost impossible to get a ruling majority in Israel without including them...so they take advantage of this and demand a steep political price, getting pretty much whatever they want. So the *Haredi* have exemptions from serving in the military as long as they don't work. And most receive a small stipend from the government.

Most of the hotels in Israel have a specially designated elevator to use on Shabbat.

For men in Israel, military service is mandatory. Active duty is from age 18 to 21, and then you are in the reserves until age 55. So for *Haredi* to keep their military exemptions, over half of them simply don't work. Rather, they just study the Old Testament and the ancient Jewish commentaries in schools called "yeshivas." Let me repeat that for emphasis, *Haredi* spend their entire lives studying religious texts full time. Understandably, some 60 percent are considered under the poverty level.

Haredi are very, very conservative as they try to keep the Old Testament Law, word for word — all 613 Jewish laws! These guys are amazing. For instance, on Shabbat, they can't do any work whatsoever. They tear up their toilet paper the day before in a little pile next to the toilet so they don't have to do work (tearing toilet paper) on Shabbat. Nor do they make or receive phone calls, drive a car, or do anything that could be considered work.

Most of the hotels in Israel have a specially designated elevator to use on Shabbat. It goes up and down all day, automatically stopping at each floor. That way the *Haredi* can use the elevator without pushing buttons—which would be considered "work."

There are approximately 150,000 unmarried ultra-Orthodox Jews in the world between the ages of 18 and 35...

The Orthodox wives cook all the food for Shabbat the day before. Also, believe it or not, many Haredi wives shave their heads so they won't look attractive to their husbands (in public they wear a wig—go figure). Grace looks pretty good, huh?

Haredi are having children at three times the rate of secular Jews. A family with 10 kids is not uncommon, and demographers now estimate about a third of last year's Jewish babies were born into the ultra-Orthodox community.

This is causing a lot of anger on the secular side because they are getting all the benefits of government, hospitals, schools, etc., but pay no taxes since they don't work.

Young, marriage-age *Haredi* do not date. Rather, eligible guys and girls meet for coffee or coke at a public place, sit across from each other and never touch. When we are traveling in Israel, we often see couples in hotel restaurants or lobbies. They spend hours talking but would never do anything close to kissing, much less hopping in the sack together. If they like each other, they continue to meet and eventually get married.

Which brings us back to the 144,000 male Jewish virgins. There are approximately 150,000 unmarried ultra-Orthodox Jews in the world between the ages of 18 and 35, the only group of Jewish men who can fulfill the prophecy.

Imagine what they will be like when, post-Rapture, God suddenly opens their eyes to Biblical truth and marks 144,000 of them for service. They already have a zeal for God's Word, so when they understand the rest of the story of how their forefathers rejected Jesus their Messiah, they will become the most proficient and prolific evangelists the world has ever seen!

God will use these guys in such a powerful way that millions of people living in the Tribulation world will rather live for Christ and die on this earth than line up with the New World Leader's agenda.

> *"After these things I looked, and behold, a great multitude, which no one could count, from every nation and all tribes and peoples and tongues . . ." Revelation 7:9*

> *"...these are the ones who come out of the great tribulation, and they have washed their robes and made them white in the blood of the Lamb." Revelation 7:14*

Bible prophecy is once again fulfilled. Mind-boggling, don't you think?

CHAPTER SIXTEEN

RAPTURE OR RETURN?

As prophesied, the Lord Jesus is coming again. First He comes in the sky to remove the Church Age Saints prior to the seven years of horrific Tribulation. Then again seven years later He comes to defeat Satan and rule from Jerusalem as King of the Earth for 1000 years.

But not everyone believes the Lord will first return to whisk away the Believers before the horrible Tribulation. They just can't seem to understand the fact that the Lord "paid it all" on the Cross. But He did. Born-again Believers have passed out of judgment:

> *"Truly, truly, I say to you, he who hears My word, and believes Him who sent Me, has eternal life, and* ***does not come into judgment****, but has passed out of death into life."* *John 5:24*

All of our sins—past, present and future—were nailed to the Cross some 2000 years ago. Whatever you did wrong yesterday, whatever you do wrong today, and whatever you do wrong in the future—all are covered by Jesus' blood atonement.

> *"When you were dead in your transgressions and the uncircumcision of your flesh, He made you alive together with Him, having forgiven us all our transgressions, having canceled out the certificate of debt consisting of decrees against us, which was hostile to us; and He has taken it out of the way, having nailed it to the cross." Col. 2:13-14*

There is nothing left for you to do, or not do, in this life. You are as cleansed as you'll ever be.

So there is nothing left for you to do, or not do, in this life. You are as cleansed as you'll ever be and ready to meet the Lord in the air just as you are. You won't have to endure the future Tribulation because God has promised you'll escape His wrath.

> *"For God has not destined us for wrath," 1Thes. 5:9a*

More than anything, we're not instructed to look down at the earth for the Antichrist, but rather to look up to heaven for Jesus Christ!

> *"Set your mind on the things above, not on the things that are on earth." Col. 3:2*

This means we're looking for the true white horse of Revelation 19:11, not the false white horse of Revelation 6:2. But the two arrivals can still be confusing. Sometimes it's hard to know which verses refer to the Rapture and which verses refer to the Return. So the following will help clear the fog.

Clear and Distinct Scriptural Differences

The clearest way to distinguish between the two is to determine if the verse in question is referring to the Lord coming "for" His saints, or "with" His saints.

For the Lord Himself will descend from heaven with a shout, with the voice of the archangel and with the trumpet of God...

Example—For His Saints:

> *"For the Lord Himself will descend from heaven with a shout, with the voice of the archangel and with the trumpet of God, and the dead in Christ will rise first. Then we who are alive and remain will be caught up together with them in the clouds to meet the Lord in the air, and so we shall always be with the Lord." 1Thes. 4:16-17*

Example—With His Saints:

> *"So that He may establish your hearts without blame in holiness before our God and Father at the coming of our Lord Jesus with all His saints." 1Thes. 3:13*

Consider these other differences in the two events:

Rapture/Translation

1. Translation of all believers.
2. Translated go to heaven.
3. Earth not judged.
4. Any moment, signless.
5. Not in the Old Testament.
6. Affects believers only.
7. Before the day of wrath.
8. No reference to Satan.
9. Comes "for" His own.
10. He comes in the air.
11. He claims His bride.
12. Only His own see Him.
13. Tribulation begins.
14. A mystery.

Second Coming/Established Kingdom

1. No translation.
2. Translated saints return to earth.
3. Earth's righteousness established.
4. Follows definite predicted signs.
5. Predicted often in the Old Testament.
6. Affects all men.
7. Concluding the day of wrath.
8. Satan bound.
9. Comes "with" His own.
10. He comes to the earth.
11. He comes with His bride.
12. Every eye will see Him.
13. Millennial kingdom begins.
14. Predicted.

These two list comparisons show in no uncertain terms that there are definitely two distinct comings, one for His Church and one with His Church.

Therefore, using the comparisons above to guide our reasoning, the following is a fairly decent list compiled by Tommy Ice and Timothy Demy (*Fast Facts on Bible Prophecy*, [Eugene: Harvest House, 1997], pp.186-187), showing the differences in the Rapture/Arrival verses compared to the Second Coming/Return verses:

Rapture Verses

John 14:1-3 - Receive you to Myself
Rom 8:19 - Revealing of God
1Cor 1:7-8 - Revelation of God
1Cor 15:51-53 - A mystery that happens in the twinkling of an eye
1Cor 16:22 - Come quickly, Lord
Phil 3:20,21 - We receive a body like Jesus
Phil 4:5 - The Lord is near
Col 3:4 - Christ revealed
1Thes 1:10 - Rescued from wrath
1Thes 2:19 - In presence of Jesus
1Thes 4:13-18 - We meet the Lord in the air
1Thes 5:9 - Not destined for wrath
1Thes 5:23 - Without blame
2Thes 2:1 - Gather together to Him
2Thes 2:3 - Apostasy comes first
Titus 2:14 - He redeems us
Heb 9:28 - We eagerly await Him
James 5:7-9 - Coming of Lord is near
1Pet 1:7,13 - The revelation

Rapture Verses, Con't

1Pet 5:4 - Shepherd appears
1John 2:28-3:2 - When He appears
Jude 21 - We wait anxiously
Rev 2:25 - Until He comes
Rev 3:10 - Kept from the hour of testing

Second Coming Verses

Ezek 21:27 - He comes Whose right it is
Dan 2:44,45 - Kingdom endures forever
Dan 7:9-14 - Kingdom never destroyed
Dan 12:1-3 - Time of distress
Zech 2:10 - Jesus will live in our midst on earth
Zech 12:10 - Him Whom they pierced
Zech 13:9 - Jews call on Jesus
Zech 14:1-15 - All nations against Jerusalem
Zech 14:4 - Jesus Stands on Mt. of Olives
Zech 14:5 - Saints come with Him
Zech 14:9 - He will be King over earth
Mal 3:1 - Comes to His Temple
Matt 13:41 - Angels gather offenders
Matt 24:15-31; -Follows the Great Tribulation
Matt 26:64 - Jesus comes in the clouds
Mark 13:14-27 - Follows the time of Tribulation
Mark 14:62 - Right hand of power
Luke 21:25-28 - Signs in sun, moon, stars precede event
Acts 1:9-11 - Jesus will come in the sky
Acts 3: 19-21 - Time of refreshing
1Thes 3:13 - Comes with His saints
2Thes 1:6-10 - Revealed from heaven
2 Thes 2:8 - Jesus defeats Satan

Second Coming Verses, Con't

1 Pet 4:12,13 - We rejoiced at His coming
2 Pet 3:1-14 - Day of God
Jude 14,15 - Lord comes with holy ones
Rev 1:7 - Every eye will see Him
Rev 19:11-20 - Heavenly armies with Him
Rev 20:1-6 - Binds Satan
Rev 22:7,12,20 - I am coming

Therefore comfort one another with these words.
1Thes. 4:18

CHAPTER SEVENTEEN

SHOULD WE CONFESS SINS FOR FORGIVENESS AFTER SALVATION?

"If we confess our sins, He is faithful and righteous to forgive us our sins and to cleanse us from all unrighteousness." 1John 1:9

The above verse may be one of the most misunderstood verses in the Bible, even for relatively solid and well-versed Believers.

At first glance, this verse seems pretty simple. "If" we confess our sins, He (Jesus) will forgive our sins and cleanse us.

Most churches today teach that this verse means we must confess our sins, ongoing, to be forgiven, that we must continually "clean the slate." An often-heard reference to this verse is, "1 John 1:9 is the Christian's 'Bar of Soap.'"

But, thankfully, this is not true. We can't self-scrub ourselves clean. Here's why not...

For this verse to mean that we have to continually confess our sins to be forgiven, as the popular interpretation implies, means that the finished work of the Cross is not finished, that Jesus didn't pay it all, and that we have an ongoing part in our personal salvation.

And what if we don't confess a sin? Do we lose our salvation? What if we forget a sin? What if we didn't know we had sinned?

Three Key Words

Under closer scrutiny of the verse, we see there are three key words that prove it could not mean that we must continually confess our sins.

The verse begins with the word, "If..." This would mean that for your sin to be forgiven, it is dependent on something that you do or do not do. It would imply a false works doctrine.... salvation based on what we do, or do not do.

What if we don't confess a sin? Do we lose our salvation? What if we forget a sin?

But that's not Scriptural. Anything to do with salvation by works contradicts other Scripture:

> *"For by grace you have been saved through faith; and that not of yourselves, it is the gift of God; not as a result of works..." Eph. 2:8,9*

"He saved us, not on the basis of deeds which we have done in righteousness, but according to His mercy, by the washing of regeneration and renewing by the Holy Spirit." Titus 3:5

The second key word is "forgive." For that verse to mean that you are not forgiven until you confess each sin is opposite what the Bible teaches... that ALL your sin was taken out of the way 2000 years ago:

You were washed, ...you were sanctified, ...you were justified in the name of the Lord Jesus Christ and in the Spirit of our God.

"Having canceled out the certificate of debt consisting of decrees against us,which was hostile to us; and He has taken it out of the way, having nailed it to the cross." Col. 2:14

The third key word is "cleanse." Does ongoing confession make you clean? Not according to other verses discussing being cleansed in the past tense:

"...those who have been sanctified by faith in Me.'" Acts 26:18b

"By this will we have been sanctified through the offering of the body of Jesus Christ once for all." Heb. 10:10

"Such were some of you; but you were washed, but you were sanctified, but you were justified in the name of the Lord Jesus Christ and in the Spirit of our God." 1Cor. 6:11

When you were saved, God the Holy Spirit came into your life *forever,* never to leave (Heb 13:5). Therefore you were fully and completely cleansed *forever* at salvation and it's unnecessary to be cleansed ever again.

Did Paul Forget?

Paul, our Church Age apostle, never mentioned ongoing confession of our sins except to one another for accountability (James 5:16). If ongoing confession was required before God forgave each of our sins, did Paul just forget to mention it in all his letters? No, he said just the opposite:

Jesus only mentions "confessing" when He was speaking to the Jews who were under the law.

> *"But now having been freed from sin and enslaved to God, you derive your benefit, resulting in sanctification, and the outcome, eternal life."*
> *Rom. 6:22*

Jesus only mentions "confessing" when He was speaking to the Jews who were under the law (Matt. 10:32).

It is also interesting to note that John wrote 1 John in 95 AD, about 50 years after the first New Testament books were originally penned. Would this be the first mention of ongoing confession for the forgiveness of sin if it were THAT important?

John did say in the verse before, 1 John 1:8, that if we say we don't have sin, we are a liar. So even if we could continually confess sin for forgiveness, the moment we confess it, we are still the same dirty rotten fleshly person we were before we confessed! Nothing would be changed!!

Self-sanctification?

Some people teach that you have "positional" sanctification at the moment of conversion but have to work for your "progressive" sanctification. This is not true—any concept of self-sanctification is from the pit of hell. All it does is yoke people with the lie that Jesus didn't do enough on the Cross and they have to do something to be more acceptable to God.

The concept of ongoing confession of sin to procure forgiveness is simply a bad doctrine holdover from the Catholic Church... just as Amillennial and anti-Jewish doctrines were initially embraced by Luther and others in the early Protestant movements.

> ***The concept of ongoing confession of sin to procure forgiveness is simply a bad doctrine.***

Then What *Is* the meaning of 1 John 1:9?

If 1 John 1:9 doesn't mean we have to continually confess our sins to be forgiven, what the heck does it mean?

In his book, *Forgiven Forever,* Hector MacLeod explains in eye-opening fashion that 1 John was written in response to the Gnostic claims of the time. And he shows that the context is actually dealing with one-time confession for individual salvation.

Yes, make no mistake about it, to be saved we ARE to confess to the Lord that we are a sinner, confessing that we know we can only escape the horrors of hell via trusting the shed blood of Jesus Christ on the Cross at Calvary.

We are certainly to acknowledge and repent of each and every sin by which we are convicted by the Holy Spirit.

And we are certainly to acknowledge and repent of each and every sin by which we are convicted by the Holy Spirit living inside us. But that is because we are already forgiven, not to earn forgiveness! Acknowledgment of sin is the natural process of spiritual maturity—growing in knowledge, faith, and the grace of our Lord.

Ongoing confession of sin to the Lord, for forgiveness, is not required... actually, we are called "foolish" for even thinking that way!

> *"Are you so foolish? Having begun by the Spirit, are you now being perfected by the flesh?" Gal. 3:3*

I will go as far to say that there is nothing one can do, or not do, to make oneself more, or less cleansed, than that which Jesus accomplished on the Cross!

Is that not just incredible? Everything that can be done has been done by our Lord. When He said, "It is finished," it was totally finished! Wow, that is just incredible!

Just a Note

Through the years while Hector was alive, we bought his book, *Forgiven Forever*, by the caseload. God has used his book to make known the true grace of God to countless individuals.

The most common remark we hear is that reading it brought them such a peaceful release!

> *"And the peace of God, which surpasses all comprehension..." Phil. 4:7*

Before Hector died at age 93, he graciously gave the rights of the book to Compass in order to keep it in circulation. We have reprinted it and also have it available both in paperback and in a free eBook format. You can download it from the compass.org store.

And reading it may very well just change your life!

CHAPTER EIGHTEEN

THE DESIGNED DECLINE OF PUBLIC EDUCATION

There comes a time when you have to call a spade a spade. Now is one of those times.

Our public schools are dead in the water. What's going on? Are they so bad they aren't even salvageable?

We'll start by taking a quick look back a few years at some of the *published* goals of the Communists to see how they're doing today.

The following are excerpts taken from the *Congressional Record, Appendix,* pp. A34-35, of the House of Representatives, January 10, 1963:

> In an effort to warn Americans of the Communist agenda in America, Congressman Herlong, from Florida, read 45 Current Communist Goals taken from the book, *The Naked Communist,* by Cleon Skousen. Published Communist Goals: (1963)

These are but a select few:

11. Promote the U.N. as the only hope for mankind.

13. Do away with all loyalty oaths.

15. Capture one or both political parties in the U.S.

17. Get control of the schools. Get control of teachers' associations. Put the party line in textbooks.

20. Infiltrate the press.

21. Gain control of key positions in radio, TV and motion pictures.

25. Break down cultural standards of morality by promoting pornography and obscenity in books, magazines, motion pictures, radio and TV.

26. Present homosexuality, degeneracy and promiscuity as "normal, natural and healthy."

27. Infiltrate the churches and replace revealed religion with social religion. Discredit the Bible and emphasize the need for intellectual maturity that does not need a "religious crutch."

28. Eliminate prayer or any phase of religious expression in schools on the grounds that it violates the principle of "separation of church and state."

31. Belittle all forms of American culture and discourage the teaching of American History.

36. Infiltrate and gain control of more unions.

40. Discredit the family as an institution. Encourage promiscuity and easy divorce.

44. Internationalize the Panama Canal.

45. Give the World Court jurisdiction over the nations and individuals alike.

We allowed our government, schools, corporations and even churches to be taken over by liberal activists pushing Communist goals.

Reading that list made the hairs on my neck stand up.

It seems that while America was building the world's most capable military machine to defeat vocal Communist threats of world domination, we allowed our government, schools, corporations, and even churches to be taken over by liberal activists pushing Communist goals.

They raised people up from the inside. Once there, they would work to destroy the American Constitution by gradually installing the Communist agenda within our legal system and separate branches of government.

This sounds hard to believe, but consider what's in the Ten Planks of the *Communist Manifesto,* written by Karl Marx in 1848:

1. Abolition of private property.

2. A heavily progressive and graduated income tax.

3. Abolition of all rights of inheritance.

4. Confiscation of the property of all emigrants and rebels.

5. A central national bank with state capital and exclusive monopoly.

6. Centralization of communication and transportation overseen by the government.

7. Factories and major production owned by government. Land cultivation controlled by government.

8. Equal rights and pay in labor for male and female.

9. Government control of population distribution around the country.

10. Free education for all children in government schools. Combine education with industrial production.

Seems by using ol' Karl's definition, we *are* a Communist nation! Someone once said, "None are more hopelessly enslaved than those who falsely believe they are free."

How did they get so far, so fast, so easily? I believe it was the #10 plank above. Our public schools are the biggest contribution to our nation's problems.

Public education in America began by seeking God as the purveyor of knowledge. Our first universities, Harvard, Princeton, Yale, etc., were all seminaries. They knew the Bible was the key to knowledge.

> *"The fear of the LORD is the beginning of knowledge;" Pro. 1:7a*

If the fear of the Lord is the beginning of wisdom, how much can a child learn if God is not an integral part of the education?

> *"Unless the LORD builds the house, they labor in vain who build it;" Psa. 127:1a*

The Bible says God's Word is the key to prosperity.

> *"But his delight is in the law of the LORD, and in His law he meditates day and night. And he will be like a tree firmly planted by streams of water, which yields its fruit in its season, and its leaf does not wither; and in whatever he does, he prospers." Psa. 1:2-3*

With all the recent school shootings, we're all understandably concerned about school safety. But, more importantly, it's our kids' spiritual foundations that are at risk. Are we trading the next life for this one?

With those kind of priorities, we shouldn't be shocked to see how many people will take the Mark of the Beast to live a little longer on this earth only to spend eternity in the black fires of hell.

Eternity is a long time. There is a God. There is a heaven and a hell. But kids are not taught that anymore and we're now paying the price.

We've lost our God-centered public schools to the godless principles of the liberal and Communist agenda. They've got control of our public schools (and a lot of private schools) and have been cranking out virtue-less children by the millions every year.

Eternity is a long time. There is a God. There is a heaven and a hell.

As the baby boomers die out, they are being replaced primarily by youth with no understanding of capitalism, no understanding of the Constitution, no understanding of the Bible, and therefore no understanding of their future.

Consider these facts:

- 30 million adult Americans who attended public school cannot read this sentence or fill out a job application.

- 50% of school kids smoke, do drugs, or drink alcohol.

- Birth control pills are offered to any student at any time without parental notification.

- 70% of all college freshmen have to take remedial classes.

- School kids are forbidden by law to name the name of Jesus in school. "Mohammad" is OK, as is "Buddha."

- Public schools are run by teachers of whom 90% vote as Democrats.

- 80% of schools admit to cheating to achieve more Federal Funding.

- Values Relativism is taught in public schools, teaching that every child must make up his or her own values. (By taking the Bible out of school as a measuring stick, they can insert homosexuality, free sex, abortion, etc.)

- Most videos shown in sex education classes are so graphic and gross that if they were found in the possession of a convicted sex offender, they would be sent back to prison for possession of pornography.

- Planned Parenthood has access to enter every public school in America, but the Bible is banned.

"How blessed is the man who does not walk in the counsel of the wicked, nor stand in the path of sinners, nor sit in the seat of scoffers!" Psa. 1:1

If God is not in our schools, then our kids are "walking in the counsel of the wicked," "standing in the path of sinners," and "sitting in the seat of scoffers."

Charles Stanley said, "When you send a child into a public school today, you're sending them into a pagan society."

The hard truth is that if our schools are *not* for God, then they *are* for Satan. And the Bible warns us that Satan brings us the opposite of a blessing.

> *"The wicked are not so, but they are like chaff which the wind drives away. Therefore the wicked will not stand in the judgment, nor sinners in the assembly of the righteous. For the LORD knows the way of the righteous, but the way of the wicked will perish."* Ps 1:4-6

Is this what we want for our children? No, but it's what we're getting. If your child or grandchild is in public school, Satan has them right where he wants them.

The hard truth is that if our schools are not for God, then they are for Satan.

It's interesting that most people rate schools as a whole with a "D" while they rate their own local school as an "A" or "B." But the Bible says a school is an "F" if God isn't there.

Our public school system is a certifiable mess. There's no reason a Believer should put their children at risk in public school. None!

CHAPTER NINETEEN

SATAN'S LIE: DO EVERYTHING JESUS SAYS

There's a lot of unnecessary heartbreak in churches today due to a misinterpretation of how to apply the Gospel accounts of Matthew, Mark, Luke, and John to the lives of Believers living in the Church Age.

Should we simply do everything Jesus says to do? Word for word? Or is a closer examination warranted? When I was a new Believer, I was told by my pastor, "If Jesus said it, I believe it and I will do it."

Well, under closer examination, that's just not the way you should apply the Gospel accounts to our lives today. When Jesus came to the earth, he was a Jew living under the Jewish law. He obeyed the law perfectly, without sin.

When Jesus addressed crowds, there were no Christians present, only Jews under the Levitical Law. Christians, or better described as Church Age Believers, only came about after Jesus' death and the arrival of God's Holy Spirit on earth Who could permanently indwell Believers. The arrival of God's Holy Spirit and His departure at the Rapture are the bookends of the Church Age (see dispensational graphic inside front cover).

Therefore, what was recorded in the Gospels are His instructions and interactions with Jews under the law. To them He said things that can't possibly be meant for Believers today. For instance, Jesus said:

To the Jews under the law, He said things that can't possibly be meant for Believers today.

"For where two or three have gathered together in My name, I am there in their midst." Matt. 18:20

If we took that verse and applied it to Believers in the Church Age, we'd have a problem. Doesn't Jesus live in my heart—even when I'm alone in the woods? Do I need to find another Believer to "gather" or be near me to ensure He is in my heart? Of course not.

Another obvious example is in Matthew 24:

"But woe to those who are pregnant and to those who are nursing babies in those days!" Matt. 24:19

Should believers be concerned about getting pregnant in the last days? Of course not. More obvious examples of Gospel verses that don't apply to us. Jesus said:

"If your right eye makes you stumble, tear it out" Matt. 5:29a

Should we poke our eyes out to stop ourselves from sinning?

> *"Are you so foolish? Having begun by the Spirit, are you now being perfected by the flesh?" Gal. 3:3*

Jesus said:

> *"...it is the one who has endured to the end who will be saved." Matt. 10:22*

Is our salvation today dependent on our endurance? Nope:

> *"He saved us, not on the basis of deeds which we have done in righteousness..." Titus 3:5*

Understanding the difference between the dispensation of Israel and the dispensation of the Church Age sheds a whole new light on the Gospels.

Jesus said:

> *"Strive to enter by the narrow door..." Luke 13:24*

Is *our* salvation today dependent on how much we strive? Of course not:

> *"...I will give to the one who thirsts from the spring of the water of life without cost." Rev. 21:6*

Jesus said:

> *"...if you do not forgive others, then your Father will not forgive your transgressions." Matt. 6:15*

Is our salvation today dependent on us forgiving others? Not a chance! In the Church Age, we're already totally forgiven of past, present, and future sin. And we are to forgive as we have been forgiven:

> *"Be kind to one another, tender-hearted, forgiving each other, just as God in Christ also* ***has forgiven*** *you."*
> *Eph. 4:32*

These verses make it obviously impossible to follow Jesus' every command. Understanding the difference between the dispensation of Israel and the dispensation of the Church Age sheds a whole new light on the Gospels and clears up why Jesus said what He did.

Believers should get their primary instructions from Paul's Epistles that were written to post-Cross Born-Again Believers.

The Old Testament and the Gospels are rich in value, but we can't apply everything Jesus said to us because Jesus was addressing Jews under the Law.

So when you study the Bible, be sure to "accurately handle the Word" (2 Tim. 2:15), and you'll be amazed how the rest of the Bible comes together!

INDEX OF SCRIPTURE

2 Corinthians

Galatians

Ephesians

Philippians

Colossians

1 Thessalonians

Revelation

A non-profit, non-denominational ministry

Biblelands Cruise

Join us on the trip of a lifetime and make your Bible come alive like never before!

STEELING THE MIND BIBLE CONFERENCE

Invest a day, reap rewards for a lifetime as top Christian speakers teach on tough Bible topics.

Whoa... who needs coffee! Start your day with a Bible verse and an eye-opening commentary.

eNews

The chapters in this book came from our monthly Compass eNews articles—get one free each month!

Creation & the Grand Canyon

Join us and learn the scientific facts about how a global flood formed the canyon only 4500 years ago.

Browse our 300+ awesome video & audio Bible studies recorded from past *Steeling the Mind Bible Conferences*.